Composition, Pedagogy & the Scholarship of Teaching

Also in the CrossCurrents series

CHARLES I. SCHUSTER, SERIES EDITOR

Composition, Pedagogy & the Scholarship of Teaching

EDITED BY DEBORAH MINTER & AMY M. GOODBURN
Preface by Ann Ruggles Gere

Boynton/Cook Publishers
HEINEMANN
Portsmouth, NH

Boynton/Cook Publishers, Inc.
A subsidiary of Reed Elsevier Inc.
361 Hanover Street
Portsmouth, NH 03801–3912
www.boyntoncook.com

Offices and agents throughout the world

© 2002 by Boynton/Cook Publishers, Inc.

Cataloging-in-Publication Data (CIP) is on file with the Library of Congress.
ISBN 0-86709-524-5

Editor: Lisa Luedeke
Series editor: Charles I. Schuster
Production service: Lisa S. Garboski, bookworks
Production coordinator: Sonja S. Chapman
Cover Design: Joni Doherty
Compositor: TechBooks
Manufacturing: Steve Bernier

Printed in the United States of America on acid-free paper
06   05   04   03   02   DA   1   2   3   4   5

Contents

Acknowledgments

This book owes its inception, in part, to a grant the editors received from the University of Nebraska-Lincoln's Teaching and Learning Center to sponsor workshops on documenting teaching and learning in college English classrooms. We were very pleased when so many of our colleagues expressed interest in, and support for, these workshops. We hope that this collection honors those conversations as well as the people and sponsoring organizations who supported them.

This project also stems from the ongoing conversations and collaborative knowledge-building with respect to teaching that our department promotes. In particular, we appreciate how our colleagues in composition—Joy Ritchie, Chris Gallagher, Malea Powell, and Robert Brooke—have helped us to explore and value our teaching as scholarly work.

We are greatly indebted to the staff at Heinemann Boynton/Cook, Chuck Schuster, the *CrossCurrents* series editor, and our research assistant, Kelly Grey.

Finally, we want to acknowledge our families' contributions to this project. Without the support of our partners, Dale Minter and Gary Czapla, and their willingness to take care of our children—Tyler, Matthew, Marissa, Benjamin, and Ethan—while we worked, this collection would not have been possible.

About the Website

On our Website, contributors to this collection share materials that represent how we have documented postsecondary teaching in composition. In sharing these materials, we hope to invite ongoing conversation about the importance of making representations of teaching public and accessible. You will find sample teaching statements, course portfolios, peer observations, student texts, job application materials, as well as guided heuristics that you might use to facilitate your own teaching documentation.

While we invite you to download these materials as you compose your own representations of teaching, we believe the site sponsors more than imitation. First, your interaction with the materials collected here furthers the state of conversations about how best to pursue and learn from the challenging work of documenting teaching. Second, the Website materials represent the contributors' efforts to articulate the scholarship of teaching in relation to composition studies. Thus, readers are invited to see how such work bears out in practice, juxtaposing contributors' claims for the material collected here with your own assessments of it. Finally, the Website materials offer insights into how composition pedagogy is documented, valued, and assessed across a range of institutional contexts. Because teaching is so important to our field, we find these artifacts vital in providing glimpses into the specific institutional contexts of our field and the conditions of work in composition. Please visit our Website at **<http://www.heinemann.com/minter-goodburn>**.

Preface
Anne Ruggles Gere

Composition Studies is a pedagogical field. The Classical Rhetoric that comprises its roots was peopled by teachers concerned with imparting strategies as well as ways of thinking about language and persuasion. Its more recent origins in the writing programs that emerged after World War II led to a body of research focused on how students write and how they can learn to do it better. It is not surprising, then, that this field has taken leadership in developing innovative teaching practices. Many of the student-centered classroom approaches now endorsed by those engaged with the scholarship of teaching movement were first introduced in composition classes.

That we are now at a place where the intellectual work of teaching receives regular and serious discussion strikes me as wonderful and remarkable. I began postsecondary teaching in 1970 as a lecturer in a poetry class required of English majors at the University of Michigan. No one asked to see my syllabus or to visit my class; the fact that I showed up in the classroom and turned in grades at the end of the semester seemed to be all that was required. When I became a graduate student instructor, I was given a few sample syllabi, and once, I think, a professor administrating the writing program visited my class. By the time I became an assistant professor, Scantron student evaluations were being used. Each semester students answered questions like "Overall this is a very good course" and "This is a very good instructor" with a five-point scale ranging from "strongly agree" to "strongly disagree." When I came up for tenure, the numbers resulting from these evaluations may have been considered, but that was the only evidence of teaching provided. It simply didn't occur to my colleagues or to me that I should be offering any other kind of teaching documentation. My promotion to full professor included a bow in the direction of teaching. In addition to more of the Scantron numbers, my file included a letter written by a colleague who had visited one of my classes and syllabi from some of my courses. When I received a university award for teaching/mentoring, former and current students wrote letters on my behalf. I presume that their letters may have included statements about my teaching, but since I wasn't allowed to see the letters, I'm not certain. In other words, my entire career has included no requirement that I make my teaching visible to anyone outside my own classes. I say this with regret, not pride, and I am delighted by the appearance of volumes like this one because they provide tangible evidence of a shift toward making teaching visible.

This volume marks another moment when Composition Studies asserts leadership in pedagogical matters. Ours is a pedagogical field *and* one that has forwarded many innovations in teaching. As Deborah Minter and Amy Goodburn note in the Introduction, the calls to document postsecondary teaching currently outnumber reflective conversations about how to evaluate and learn from representations of teaching. The essays included here offer a variety of perspectives on how teaching can be made visible to many audiences for multiple purposes. One of the most urgent, but not necessarily most important, uses of such visibility is in the area of assessment. Rendering teaching available to the scrutiny of others makes it possible to evaluate classroom work, both for one's own purposes and for consideration by others; it ceases to be a private activity enacted behind the closed classroom door. Perhaps more important, making teaching visible assigns it a different status in the academy; it can be held up, as can a series of publications, when individuals are being considered in high-stakes decisions like hiring, tenure, or promotion. Most important, making teaching visible enhances its capacity for knowledge-making. The oft-quoted refrain "we who teach learn twice" takes on new meaning when we consider the intellectual dimensions of scrutinizing teaching, both our own and that of others.

The emphasis on rendering pedagogy in forms that make scrutiny possible demonstrates this volume's connection to the scholarship of teaching. In addition to establishing a link between composition studies and the scholarship of teaching, this collection provides a wide-angle view of how we portray and value teaching at the beginning of the 21st century. These days job candidates, both those I help to screen and those I help to prepare for the market, are asked to offer representations of their teaching. For some this means making a "pedagogical presentation" as part of a campus visit, but more commonly it means putting together a teaching portfolio. Reading this book has helped me think differently about these portfolios.

Portfolios, I've come to understand, are not all created equal. Even distinctions like formative and summative purposes for portfolio evaluation do not hold. Despite their theoretical usefulness, formative and summative evaluation can never be hermetically sealed off from one another where teaching portfolios are concerned. The reflection and intellectual growth of instructors who consider the implications of their own classroom practices can never be entirely separated from the evaluative gaze of colleagues and administrators charged with making decisions about an individual's professional future.

Audiences for portfolios are also variable. In some cases they are known to the person creating the teaching portfolio, and in others they are complete strangers. Depending upon their position and stake in the situation, audiences read the same portfolio very differently. This reminds me to remind my graduate students to call upon the resources of rhetoric in order to remain vigilantly aware of the multiple audiences for their teaching portfolios.

Although most of the articles in this collection focus on some aspect of teaching portfolios, a few look in other directions. From these I learned to think differently about classroom observations, collaborative teaching, and the *ways* we collect and analyze the materials that comprise a portfolio. Taken together, the articles here deliver on the promise of editors Minter and Goodburn in the Introduction when they claim "attention to the scholarship of teaching can promote individual and collective development while also challenging the field of composition to take a more visible place in conversations about how to assess and improve upon postsecondary teaching."

But that's not all. To read this collection without looking at the Website would be to miss one of its most significant contributions. The authors of individual chapters show great courage and trust in sharing materials from their own portfolios as well as their classrooms, and we owe them gratitude for that alone. Furthermore, by sharing artifacts from their own teaching, the authors perform their own argument about the importance and value of making pedagogy accessible to scrutiny and assessment. They show how we can begin to discern and value the kind of knowledge teaching documentation makes available to both writer and reader.

The materials available on the Website offer models for emulation. A new assistant professor who wants to see the syllabi of others, someone facing a third-year review or consideration for tenure who wants to know more about how to make a case for his or her teaching, a senior professor who wants to offer helpful suggestions to a junior colleague mentee about representing student work—these and many others will find helpful examples on the Website. And there are other possibilities, too. In addition to answering the question "what does one look like?" for those relatively unfamiliar with representations of teaching, the Website materials offer more experienced practitioners an opportunity to think through the range of questions they might pursue through the process of documenting their teaching. The Website materials also provide an occasion for comparative interpretation. That is, readers can look at an individual author's claims about his or her teaching and then consider these in light of the artifacts included on the site. This can lead to interesting discussions about the complexities and challenges of interpreting and assessing representations of teaching. Finally, the materials on the Website give us a valuable indication of where we are as a field. By looking at how composition instruction is being documented, we can learn something about what is being valued across a range of institutional contexts and how the working conditions in composition vary.

Like scholarship of other sorts, representations of teaching provide more than evidence of prior teaching performances. They participate in the production of knowledge by calling upon others' efforts and by providing the means for future generations to build on their work. As the related fields of composition studies and the scholarship of teaching move forward, this volume offers a model from which we can benefit and to which we can contribute by offering representations of our own teaching that—like those gathered here—take seriously the opportunities for responsive and responsible scholarly work that are made available through increasingly common requirements to document our work as composition teachers.

Introduction: Why Document Postsecondary Teaching?

Deborah Minter and Amy M. Goodburn

This volume addresses a practical and disciplinary problem facing many in our field: that *calls* by administrators and scholars to document postsecondary teaching typically outstrip reflective *conversations about* how to assess, evaluate, and learn from these representations of teaching practices. Recent studies suggest increased attention to and interest in documenting classroom practice in hiring and promotion decisions. Reporting on the results of a recent survey of 740 four-year, liberal arts colleges, Seldin et al. (1999) found that evidence of effective classroom teaching is a major factor in evaluating overall faculty performance. Moreover, the authors identified significant changes across time in the practices of assessing teaching at the responding institutions. From 1978 to 1998, the use of four sources of information about teaching—systematic student ratings, faculty self-evaluations, classroom observations, and course documents such as syllabi, exams, course assignments, and so on—increased by 20 percent or more. Roughly 88 percent of college deans responding in 1998 reported using systematic student ratings in assessing teaching performance (as compared to 54.8 percent in 1978). The use of classroom visits to assess college teaching had increased from 14.3 percent to 40.3 percent over the same period. The use of faculty self-evaluations increased from 36.6 percent in 1978 to 58.7 percent in 1998. The use of course materials to evaluate teaching performance increased from 13.9 percent in 1978 to 38.6 percent in 1998. "It would seem," the authors write, "that the information-gathering process is becoming more structured and systematic, and that more colleges are reexamining and diversifying their approach to evaluating classroom teaching" (15). While similar data for research institutions is unavailable, the 1993 National Study of Postsecondary Faculty reveals that nearly 80 percent of faculty teaching in research and Ph.D.-granting institutions believe that teaching should be "a salient standard for promotion"—up somewhat significantly from the 69 percent of faculty who responded similarly in a 1989 survey (Finkelstein et al. 1998, 86).

Additional markers of this interest in attending to postsecondary teaching include the many statements and study groups initiated by professional organizations and funding agencies. At the national level, Ernest Boyer's 1990 *Scholarship Reconsidered* (issued by the Carnegie Foundation for the Advancement of Teaching) explicitly sought to "reformulate the tired debate about teaching *versus* research" (Edgerton et al., 1) by reconceptualizing faculty work into four areas of scholarship including the now widely cited "scholarship of teaching." Two groups formed from these calls include The Carnegie Academy for the Scholarship on Teaching and Learning (CASTL)[1] and the American Association for Higher Education (AAHE) Peer Review Project. Yet, as Richard Gebhardt (1997) demonstrates in his introduction to *Academic Advancement in Composition Studies,* efforts to broaden the definition of scholarship and reconceptualize teaching as scholarly work were underway prior to Boyer's 1990 publication from a variety of influential organizations and agencies, including the National Endowment for the Humanities, National Council of Teachers of English (including the college section, CCCC), the Modern Language Association, the cross-disciplinary Institutional Priorities and Faculty Rewards Project (with representatives from MLA, CCCC, and fourteen other scholarly and professional associations), and AAUP.

In response to these national efforts and pressures, postsecondary teachers increasingly have been called to document, assess, and make public their teaching practices. A primary goal of this movement is to establish teaching as a form of scholarship equivalent to and documented in the vein of traditional research activities. For instance, Lee Shulman (1993) asserts that the scholarship of teaching entails an account of some or all of the full act of teaching that is subject to peer review and accessible for use by peers in one's professional community. Similarly, Charles Glassick, Mary Huber, and Gene Maeroff (1997) outline six standards for evaluating the scholarship of teaching derived from criteria for good research: clear goals, adequate preparation, appropriate methods, significant results, effective presentation, and reflective critique. To assist teachers in this work, publications such as *The Teaching Portfolio: Capturing the Scholarship in Teaching, The Teaching Portfolio: A Practical Guide to Improved Performance and Promotion/Tenure Decisions,* and *Opening Lines: Approaches to the Scholarship of Teaching and Learning* have showcased various genres that teachers are using to represent their pedagogy. Such genres include formal teaching portfolios, peer observations, teaching philosophy statements, course portfolios, critical commentaries, and self-evaluations of individual courses, just to name a few.

Of course, the field of composition has long contributed to making visible representations of postsecondary teaching. With its focus on theorizing the production of texts and representations of practice, composition has been an important disciplinary site of claims for the value of written reflection about teaching (Bishop 1991, Gallagher and Gray in response to Yagelski 2001, Harris 1997, Yancey 1998) and for narratives about how teachers and students construct identities in classrooms (Bleich 1998, Newkirk 1997, Trimmer 1997, Ritchie and Wilson 2000). Yet many of these representations have remained situated within composition specifically, and have not yet informed (as thoroughly as

---

1. CASTL's three main programs are 1) The Teaching Academy Campus Program, 2) the Carnegie Teaching Fellow Program, and 3) scholarly/professional society connections. In addition, CASTL is developing new media/technology initiatives to advance the scholarship of teaching and learning. For more information, see *www.carnegiefoundation.org/CASTL/ highered/index.htm.*

they might) those larger and more general conversations at the national level about postsecondary teaching, or the scholarship of teaching movement, more particularly.

Two areas of inquiry where the scholarship of teaching movement might be more visibly connected to composition are 1) the field's scholarship on the development, uses, and assessment of portfolios, and 2) the field's commitment and contribution to teacher research. For the past thirty years, compositionists have used portfolios to foster student ownership over their literate practices and texts, and to facilitate assessment and evaluation of students' literacies (Belanoff and Dickson 1991, Yancey and Weiser 1997). While portfolio-based pedagogies and assessment practices within the field initially featured portfolios primarily as venues for writing (and reflection on writing), composition scholars—perhaps due to the field's responsibility for preparing teachers of writing—have long recognized the value of portfolios as a means of documenting and reflecting on teaching practices in composition (Anson 1994, Bishop 1991, Black 1997, Lyons 1998). Similarly and more recently, the teacher research movement within composition has illuminated how scenes of learning and teaching within writing classrooms can be documented in ways that expand and deepen our understanding of literacy learning as well as particular pedagogical approaches (Ray 1993, Fleischer 2000, Lee 2000).

As composition teachers who have long shared a commitment to teaching as a site of scholarly work and sought to move that commitment to the center of our work with teachers, we often looked for useful models of how others document their teaching. We were surprised to discover so little cross-conversation between the scholarship of teaching movement and composition studies. In conceptualizing how composition might inform the national conversation about scholarship of teaching, then, we considered the following questions: How does our understanding of textuality inform our representations of the classroom? How do theories of collaboration inform the construction of teaching portfolios, which are conceived in primarily individualistic terms? What do our theories of reading mean for how we read our representations of teaching? We looked for texts that would address such questions, for ourselves and for the teachers with whom we work. Conversely, cross-conversation between the scholarship of teaching movement and composition studies could extend current efforts, within the field, to understand the various ways in which composition is situated institutionally. That is, while the field has long trained ethnographic eyes on writing classrooms for the purposes of disciplinary knowledge-building (and this volume grows out of our belief that such work has much to contribute to more general discussions of documenting teaching), we believe that the field of composition studies, itself, could benefit from fuller examinations of the process of representing composition teaching for multiple purposes (including such institution-specific purposes as employment and promotion).

Such scholarly conversations could assist writing teachers in a variety of postsecondary institutions with the many kinds of intellectual work surrounding the representation of teaching writing. Graduate teaching assistants, for example, might use such texts to think about how to document their teaching for prospective employers even as they facilitate reflection on their own professional commitments. Pretenure faculty in a workshop setting might glean, from such texts, ideas about how to document their teaching for tenure processes and how to place their work in a collective dialogue about the connections across teaching, research, and service that one can make visible in such documentation. Tenured faculty might be better prepared for the challenges entailed in reading and assessing the scholarship of teaching for promotion, tenure, and merit decisions. Writing program administrators might draw on such texts in order to facilitate teacher and program development. Finally, postsecondary composition teachers, more generally, might better understand how the work of documenting our teaching makes visible for us the various constraints within which we work and the commitments we share.

Composition, Pedagogy, and the Scholarship of Teaching describes composition teachers (graduate students to full professors) who have documented their teaching within varying contexts and for different purposes (job searches, promotion/tenure processes, ongoing professional development, curricular/programmatic revision). As we have suggested, our focus on composition teachers is especially important to this collection because we believe there is value in thinking about how the documentation of teaching is necessarily implicated in and reflective of larger disciplinary claims, debates, and issues within composition. Thus, the book is divided into two sections. Part I addresses pragmatic issues concerning the documentation of teaching with essays on developing teaching philosophy statements, conducting classroom and peer observations, preparing course portfolios and teaching portfolios, and collecting data about teaching and students' learning. These chapters foreground the practical and intellectual dimensions involved in preparing documentation about teaching and discuss some of the issues that arise when teachers do this work. Part II focuses more specifically on how representations of teaching are read, assessed, and evaluated. These chapters focus on developing responsible methods for assessing the scholarship of teaching, critiquing the individualism inherent in many privileged forms of documentation; using teaching documentation for curricular and programmatic development; and, exploring the ethical issues involved in writing and reading such texts.

The essays collected here reflect a complex set of responses to calls for teaching documentation. Some contributors present concrete strategies that they use to represent and reflect upon their teaching (Newton et al.; Robbins; Robinson et al.). Others focus on their own teaching growth and development as sponsored by institutionally mandated forms of documentation (Goodburn, Minter, Mirtz, O'Neill). A third set of contributors attend to larger departmental and institutional cultures surrounding the documentation of teaching (Anson and Dannels; LeCourt; Schendel and Newton). Not surprisingly, many of the contributors interrogate some of the underlying assumptions inherent in local and/or national calls to document postsecondary teaching. However, some of the contributors to this volume place these questions at the center of their text. Willard-Traub, for example, questions the primacy of teachers' voices in the work of documenting classrooms. Still others probe the ethics of requiring and evaluating the documentation of postsecondary (Fox, Leverenz).

A primary strength of this collection is its focus on the practice of documenting teaching and its inclusion of "real-world" examples of how such documentation has been read, assessed, and evaluated. Our Website offers examples of teachers documenting their work in a variety of forms for different contexts and purposes. This combination foregrounds both the opportunities that teacher documentation makes possible (for individual teacher development, curricular revision, departmental and institutional reforms) and also the risks entailed in making such teaching practices visible for examination, critique, and review. Ultimately, we believe that this book emphasizes a vital but oft-overlooked precept: that documenting teaching requires not only making visible our teaching practices, but also *making arguments* about the importance and significance of such representations for other audiences. We hope this collection functions as such an argument, illuminating how attention to the scholarship of teaching can promote individual and collective development while also challenging the field of composition to take a more visible place in conversations about how to assess and improve upon postsecondary teaching.

PART I

Practical Concerns in Documenting Teaching

1

Reconsidering and Reassessing Teaching Portfolios: Reflective and Rhetorical Functions

Camille Newton, Tracy Singer, Amy D'Antonio,
Laura Bush, and Duane Roen

In the first portion of this essay, we establish a foundation for teaching portfolios by using Ernest Boyer's (1990) four categories of scholarship in *Scholarship Reconsidered*. In the second portion of our essay, we explain and illustrate how the six criteria in Charles Glassick, Mary Huber, and Gene Maeroff's (1997) publication, *Scholarship Assessed*, can be applied to evaluate teaching and teaching portfolios in ways that benefit the principle stakeholders: the faculty member, the program, the department, the institution, the students, and the tax-paying public supporting higher education.

In our discussion we explore how, through teaching portfolios, teachers address the complex tension between the reflective and rhetorical demands of constructing a teaching identity for audiences such as hiring committees and review boards, and how such use may help institutions to value teaching—and teaching identities—in the ways that Ernest Boyer recommends. We also consider the more specific case of how a teacher may, using a teaching portfolio, negotiate the tensions between adopting a professional identity determined by institutional values and constructing a professional identity through negotiation of contextual discourses. We conclude with a call for more research into how teachers' negotiations of various discourses about scholarship might have importance for our continued use of teaching portfolios as a means of developing faculty and the scholarship of teaching.

Strategies for Balancing Reflective and Rhetorical Functions of Teaching Portfolios

One of the more difficult tasks facing a junior scholar constructing a teaching portfolio is balancing the reflective function and the rhetorical function of the portfolio and each of its components. On the one hand, the portfolio offers unparalleled opportunities for fully understanding one's instructional practices—opportunities for becoming the kind of reflective practitioner that Donald Schön (1991) describes. On the other hand, representing that reflective practice to others (for example, hiring, annual review, and promotion/tenure committees) is a delicate rhetorical task—one that entails the following kinds of questions: What sort of *ethos* does the rhetor aim to establish? How does the rhetor establish that *ethos* most effectively? What counts as *logos* for the readers of the portfolio? What sort(s) of *pathos* does the rhetor aim to evoke? How does the rhetor evoke the desired *pathos* in a reader?

One strategy for balancing these dual functions is to respond to Ernest Boyer's call to blur the boundaries that have long occupied the academy and preoccupied those of us who consider ourselves academicians. Rather than view scholarship as something distinct from service, teaching, and administration, Boyer argues that scholarship must be defined broadly enough to encompass the full range of academic work—work that serves not only the academy but also society in general.

In Boyer's scheme, the scholarly work of the professoriate has four interrelated functions: discovery, integration, application, and teaching. The scholarship of discovery is what academics traditionally consider research to be: investigation for its own sake. We rarely need to convince newcomers of the importance of constructing researcher identities because their graduate professors relentlessly promote this form of scholarship. However, we might urge teacher-scholars to construct their identities in the portfolio as inquirers/discovers in such a way that they align themselves with the theoretical stances they find appealing. We should caution them, however, that constructing identities that rely heavily on theory can be hazardous, especially if those identities seem rigid and dogmatic to hiring, annual review, or promotion/tenure committees and others who make decisions about their career paths.

There can be great tension between the reflective function and the rhetorical function of the teaching portfolio. For example, a scholar may use Marxist theory as a lens for contemplating curriculum and pedagogy. In her teaching portfolio, that scholar wants to use the same lens for articulating her contemplations of instruction. How does she successfully accomplish both the reflective and rhetorical tasks that lie before her? If she explicitly labels her instruction as "Marxist" in the philosophy statement in her teaching portfolio, she may be reflecting accurately on what she does in the classroom, but hiring or annual review or promotion/tenure committees may interpret that label in unpredictable ways. Among other things, the term "Marxist" is so broad in scope that it is difficult for any reader to know precisely how a portfolio constructor is using it. To fulfill the rhetorical task, then, the scholar-teacher needs to find language that describes/explains what she does in the classroom. Such language in this case might include "critical thinking" and "critical pedagogy"—to offer two possible phrases. Rather than listing the theorists and titles that shape the scholar-teacher's self-reflection (for example, citing Paulo Freire or his *Pedagogy of the Oppressed* (1968)), the scholar-teacher points to specific parts of the relevant theories, describing her pedagogy as the antithesis of the "banking concept," which she also defines.

The following brief narrative further illustrates the tension that exists between the reflective and rhetorical functions of teaching portfolios. An acquaintance of ours, a well-rounded scholar in the Boyerian sense, was considered for promotion and tenure at another university. After the department promotion and tenure committee had reviewed his materials, members of the committee wrote a letter indicating that they had voted unanimously to recommend that he be granted tenure and promoted to the rank of associate professor. The department chair wrote an equally supportive letter. However, when the college committee finished reviewing those same materials, along with the supporting departmental letters, they wrote a letter indicating that they had voted unanimously to deny tenure and promotion. Later, the university committee, ignoring the decision of the college committee, voted unanimously to grant tenure.

So what happened in this case? The department committee members knew and valued our acquaintance and the full range of his work—in all four of Boyer's categories. Members of the college committee, though, did not know our acquaintance, and they focused on his scholarship of discovery, which they devalued because it dealt with students' writing and with writing pedagogy. They deemed writing pedagogy and students' writing as unworthy foci of inquiry. Fortunately for our acquaintance, the university committee comprised faculty from many disciplines, who, collectively, held a more Boyerian view of what counts as scholarship. They also were more removed from the disciplinary wars that rage within departments and colleges. The university committee did not see our colleague as a "compositionist" in the same way that college committee members saw him as a "compositionist." While composition often can have little value in English departments because of its overtly practical applications, it can have much elsewhere in the university for the very same reason.

Boyer defines the second category, the scholarship of integration, as "making connections across the disciplines, placing the specialties in larger context, illuminating data in a revealing way, often educating nonspecialists, too" (18). Encouraging this kind of "connectedness" and "multidisciplinary work" (19) can be more of a challenge because junior colleagues, especially in their first year of graduate school, often feel that they need to develop narrow professional identities specific to their disciplines. Pursuing interdisciplinarity sometimes can make a young scholar feel fragmented.

Sara, for example, is a Ph.D. student in conservation biology. She believes strongly that responsibly managing wildlife means managing people as much as or more than it means managing animals. Her research and professional goals are focused on exploring the intersections between the land, its animals, and the people who live and work with both. As a result, she finds significant connections between the inquiry and research in her own field and the inquiry and research in the fields of anthropology, history, law, and political science. Sara frequently shares her insights and research with students and faculty in the anthropology department, and she values the perspectives that they are able to offer to her.

Sara's belief in and commitment to interdisciplinary inquiry shows up clearly in her statement of teaching philosophy. She writes, in part:

> Conservation biology needs people who understand the multiple dimensions and complexity of problems in conservation biodiversity. This includes both a rigorous scientific background and an understanding of social dimensions of protecting natural resources. Biologists need a working knowledge of society, culture, economics, law, and politics. The ability to think critically across multiple disciplines aids in effective problem solving.
>
> I believe this is an important consideration when developing course-work for undergraduates in conservation biology and natural resource management. Students need to develop good problem-solving skills and an ability to think across disciplinary boundaries. They need the skills to communicate effectively with professionals in other disciplines. I have taught both technical courses (geographic information systems, statistics for wildlife) and non-technical courses (wildlife ecology, conservation biology, introductory biology) for majors and non-majors. Although I employ different teaching strategies for the various courses I have taught, I maintain a focus on real-world applications and problem solving in all my courses. I want to help the students to develop critical-thinking skills and to be able to discourse with professionals from other fields effectively.

Sara is energized and motivated by the connections that she has made between the values and inquiry of her department and the department of anthropology. However, she is frustrated by what she has expressed as her department's general lack of recognition and appreciation for the research in the anthropology department. Her department members' inability or refusal to value and pursue a "scholarship of integration" causes her to question her own identity and position in her discipline.

With the scholarship of application, Boyer's third category, the scholar-teacher asks, "How can knowledge be responsibly applied to consequential problems?" and "Can social problems *themselves* (Boyer's emphasis) define an agenda for scholarly investigation?" (21). What may be most important to consider here is Boyer's observation that "[n]ew intellectual understandings can arise out of the very act of application. . . . In such activities . . . theory and practice vitally interact, and one renews the other" (23). To demonstrate the scholarship of application in a portfolio, a teacher-scholar might write about ways in which she or he applies disciplinary knowledge while working in the community. In English studies, of course, there are many opportunities to apply our specialized literacy skills to benefit those who never enter the academy— for example, facilitating a writing group that meets regularly at a local public library.

The fourth category, the scholarship of teaching, describes teachers' crucial work with students. Boyer reminds us that "good teaching means that faculty, as scholars, are also learners" (24). Effective teaching requires that "[p]edagogical procedures must be carefully planned, continuously examined, and relate directly to the subject taught" (23–4). The teaching portfolio offers us opportunities to demonstrate how we make our teaching effective—how we make it a scholarly enterprise and how we make it central to our professional identities.

For most faculty in the United States, Boyer's fourth category of scholarship—teaching—represents the biggest portion of our contractual obligations to the colleges and universities that hire us. While many of us earn our doctorates at Doctoral/Research Extensive or Doctoral/Research Intensive Universities (as defined in the recently revised Carnegie designations), relatively few of us spend our careers in such institutions for the simple reason that there are relatively few large research universities in the country. (The categories are described at the Website for the Carnegie Foundation for the Advancement of Teaching: *http://www.carnegiefoundation.org./Classification/index.htm*.) Far more common are Master's Colleges and Universities or Baccalaureate Colleges, with teaching loads of three or even four course sections a semester, and Associate's Colleges, which can have even heavier teaching loads. Given the justifiable emphasis that boards of trustees, boards of regents, state legislatures, and the general public place on documenting the quality of undergraduate instruction, it is not surprising that increasingly more ads in the *MLA Job Information List* and the *Chronicle of Higher Education* request teaching portfolios (or some of their components) as items to be included in job applications.

The aforementioned external expectations can usefully inform the construction of professional identities in teaching portfolios. For instance, a young scholar in the humanities who constructs a monolithic identity as a scholar of inquiry limits his access to employment in a range of institutions. Likewise, a young scholar who constructs a monolithic identity as a scholar of teaching also limits her access to employment in a range of institutions. As mentors, we might encourage junior colleagues to construct flexible professional identities with some reasonable balance among the four kinds of scholarship that Boyer describes. Throughout our careers, the balance may shift for a variety of reasons. For instance, a research fellowship might encourage a scholar to focus entirely on inquiry for a year. Or a new opportunity to team-teach an interdisciplinary course might encourage an intense commitment to both the scholarship of integration and teaching. Successful mentors work to help graduate students understand their potential future professional identities—their identities after graduate school.

Junior scholars can also be urged to construct in their teaching portfolios not only academic/professional identities but also personal and civic ones. Here, too, a balance is important. At some institutions, the academic/professional identities are privileged so much that personal and civic identities are all but excluded. At other institutions, there is more room for the personal and the civic. Rather than considering an institution as an audience based solely on its Carnegie Foundation's designation, we posit that the acceptance of a portfolio author's multiple identities may be significantly related to the institution's comfort with its status identity implied by its designation. An institution that is insecure about its status—its Carnegie designation—will obsess over what faculty need to do for the institution to maintain that status or, more often, to achieve the next rung on the Carnegie ladder. The more insecure an institution is about its status, the more it is impressed upon faculty that they need to focus on research at the expense of everything else. For example, if a school with Doctoral/Research Intensive status is striving for an identity described as "the Harvard of the West," faculty within that institution may feel inhibited from constructing identities that include the personal and/or the civic.

A Matrix for Constructing and Assessing Portfolios

As Glassick et al. argue in *Scholarship Assessed*, universities "must fulfill a more well-rounded mission" (10) if they are to maintain their vitality and if they are to serve the larger culture. For universities to become more well-rounded in discovery, integration, application, and teaching, they must encourage faculty— new and veteran—to expand their repertoire in such areas. Teaching portfolios offer opportunities for faculty not only to demonstrate such breadth but also to negotiate the fault line between the reflective and rhetorical tasks inherent in portfolio construction.

In extending Boyer's reconsideration of what it means to do scholarly work, Glassick et al. offer six criteria for assessing scholarship. After surveying more than eight hundred chief academic officers of universities and colleges in the United States, they synthesized their findings to construct six criteria: "Clear Goals," "Adequate Preparation," "Appropriate Methods," "Significant Results," "Effective Presentation," and "Reflective Critique."

To illustrate the intersection of Boyer's four categories and Glassick et al.'s six criteria, we offer the following matrix.

		Four Categories of Academic Scholarship Boyer, 1990			
		Teaching	Integration	Application	Discovery
Six Criteria for Assessing Scholarship Glassick, Huber, Maeroff, 1997	Clear Goals				
	Adequate Preparation				
	Appropriate Methods				
	Significant Results				
	Effective Presentation				
	Reflective Critique				

Clear Goals   Glassick, Huber, and Maeroff pose three questions to determine whether the scholar has established clear goals: "Does the scholar state the basic purposes of his or her work clearly? Does the scholar define objectives that are realistic and achievable? Does the scholar identify important questions in the field?" (25). For the purposes of the discussion here, we have recast the original questions so that they encourage more generative, reflective thinking about both teaching and representations of teaching: How can I state the basic purposes of my teaching? What are some realistic and achievable goals and objectives for my teaching? What are some important questions for students to explore in my courses—or in their theses or dissertations? How do I represent the learning that results from exploring those questions?

For example, our colleague Greg Glau, Director of Writing Programs at Arizona State University, values the learning goals articulated in the Council of Writing Program Administrators Outcomes Statement (*http://www.mwsc.edu/ ~outcomes/*). Throughout the semester, he discusses the WPA Outcomes Statement with his students, and his students use the Statement as they construct course portfolios to represent their learning. In his own teaching portfolio, Greg includes samples from students' course portfolios to document that students are achieving the learning goals for the course.

Adequate Preparation   Glassick, Huber, and Maeroff offer the following questions to assess the scholar's preparation: "Does the scholar show an understanding of existing scholarship in the field? Does the scholar bring the necessary skills to his or her work? Does the scholar bring together the resources necessary to move the project forward?" (27). Again, we have recast the original questions: What is my understanding of existing scholarship on teaching? What skills do I bring to my teaching? What resources can I use to promote learning?

For example, Laura L. Bush (2001) explains in her teaching philosophy how thorough preparation offers her the opportunity to be flexible and spontaneous in the classroom, especially when the unexpected occurs:

> Even though memorable teaching moments such as these can never be planned, I believe that thorough preparation before and after teaching a class creates the possibility for positive outcomes to occur. Furthermore, I believe my own best teaching grows out of the effort that I expend to make teaching appear effortless. Preparing to run a seamless class has been especially important as I develop materials for teaching composition and literature in classrooms with computers. On the surface, technology may make my classroom appear more inviting to today's college-aged students. Yet technology may also make my classroom appear more intimidating and difficult as well. From the perspective of a teacher, technology has rewarded me with increased student-to-student and student-to-teacher interaction. However, it has also increased the complexity of my teaching, requiring added effort from me to achieve the rigorous but relaxed atmosphere that I strive to foster in any classroom.

Appropriate Methods   Here Glassick, Huber, and Maeroff's defining questions are straightforward: "Does the scholar use methods appropriate to the goals? Does the scholar apply effectively the methods selected? Does the scholar modify procedures in response to changing circumstances?" (28). Our revisions: What methods can I use to achieve the learning goals for the course? How can I effectively apply the selected teaching strategies? How can I modify my teaching in response to changing circumstances?

For instance, a new teaching assistant, prior to a classroom observation, requested that the observer—a lecturer in the department—provide feedback on whether she was meeting the goal of motivating students to be responsible for their own learning. Essentially, she wanted to know whether her methods were being applied effectively and how she might adapt future class meetings accordingly. In her observation, the lecturer wrote of the new teacher: ". . . she is exceptionally well-organized, clear to [students] about what her direction is, and prepared to move her students through a classroom activity in a purposeful way. Some students may need a bit more time than others to 'get' some activities, and there may be moments when being *less* efficient might be useful." Although the evaluation seemed positive enough, the junior colleague was not comfortable including the evaluation—or the lesson that was associated with it—in her portfolio for teaching assistant training because she had not yet been able to apply the evaluator's comments in a favorable, validated way.

Significant Results   Glassick, Huber, and Maeroff focus on pragmatic considerations in posing questions that assess the results of the scholar's work:

"Does the scholar achieve the goals? Does the scholar's work add consequentially to the field? Does the scholar's work open additional areas for further exploration?" (29). How am I helping students achieve the intended learning goals? How do my teaching practices, my scholarly teaching, and my scholarship of teaching add consequentially to students' learning, as well as to the field? How is my teaching opening additional areas for further exploration for students?

Here, we recall the example of Greg Glau, whose students illustrate the goals that they have achieved in their course portfolios.

Effective Presentation   Glassick, Huber, and Maeroff rhetorically examine the effectiveness of the scholar's work: "Does the scholar use a suitable style and effective organization to present his or her work? Does the scholar use appropriate forums for communicating work to its intended audiences? Does the scholar present his or her message with clarity and integrity? (32)." Once again, we recast their questions: How are my style and organization affecting students' learning? What forums are most appropriate for communicating not only with students but also with other stakeholders? How can I further enhance clarity and integrity of my communication with students and others? How can I be most rhetorically effective in my teaching portfolio?

For example, consider again the new teaching assistant who, before her observation, had also requested feedback on whether she was meeting the goal of communicating her teaching philosophy through classroom practices. In that same observation, the lecturer also wrote: "...I would have to characterize her behavior towards students as respectful but firm.... My observation suggests that [this teacher] is indeed running a student-focused classroom but one where the teacher has not given up the prerogative of her authority...." Although the evaluation seemed positive enough, the TA was again hesitant to include the write-up in her online teaching portfolio a year later, as a link to the department Website. The administration seemed to advocate assuming the mantle of teaching and throwing off the robe of authority simultaneously. The new teacher did not understand the department's position, reinforced by the identity constructed for her in the prior evaluation. The tension between reflective and rhetorical practice for this teacher is characterized by the fact that, despite a potentially favorable view from an administrative audience, she felt that mirroring the department's values was not rhetorically appropriate for an Internet audience.

Perhaps gaining confidence from her teaching philosophy's brief review of rhetorical theory and scholarship supporting her approach, teaching assistant Amy D'Antonio explains her method of synthesizing her department's advocated method with her own practices:

> I consider my role in the classroom community not as that of an instructor, but rather as that of a reminder. I accomplish my reminding not only through declining authority, but also through actively allocating it to the students

themselves. For example, when we discuss progress on writing assignments, I always ask first what successes students have had, then what difficulties they are experiencing. The students are then in the position to give and receive advice and to share writing strategies among themselves. Such continual peer teaching prepares my students to sympathize with each others' successes and difficulties, to offer authoritative advice and encouragement, and to develop and articulate insights into their relationships with each other. Thus, they become adept at presenting their own perspectives within a conscious framework of multiple points of view.

Reflective Critique   The last criterion in Glassick, Huber, and Maeroff's list implies the following questions: "Does the scholar critically evaluate his or her own work? Does the scholar bring an appropriate breadth of evidence to his or her critique? Does the scholar use evaluation to improve the quality of future work? (34)". Our revisions: How can I critically evaluate my teaching most effectively? What breadth of evidence do I need to bring to my critique? How can I best use evaluation to improve the quality of future teaching? Once more we return to our colleague Greg Glau, who carefully analyzes students' course portfolios to assess how much they are learning. If the learning in some areas is not as substantial as it is in other areas, Greg refocuses some instruction the following semester.

These questions seem to speak directly to the use of teaching portfolios. As our previous examples illustrate, teachers are encouraged to reflect upon and evaluate their teaching as they collect, construct, and select the documents that they will include in their teaching portfolios. Such reflection and evaluation ideally leads to better future teaching. And the administrators and hiring committees who read teaching portfolios reflect upon and evaluate the scholarship of those who submit portfolios; ideally, they review their program practices and the goals and views of scholarship in light of such documents.

Clearly, teaching portfolios have the potential to encourage reflection, evaluation, and improvement in teaching and in the scholarship of teaching. They are powerful tools. As always, we need to critically explore our use of such tools in order to use them ethically and effectively. Our intent in this essay has been to explore instructors' negotiations of the tensions between the various discourses about scholarship within which they work as they construct teaching selves in the teaching portfolio. In many ways, this is a negotiation between voices that are distinct and sometimes alien—in Bakhtin's (1981) sense of "alien" where *svoj,* one's own word or one's own worldview, stands in contrast with *cuzoj,* the word or worldview of another or the "alien word" (427).

Teachers who construct teaching portfolios produce reflective documents about their teaching (and their "developing" teaching identities) and provide "evidence" (in the forms of vitas, syllabi, lesson plans, student evaluations, and the like) to support their reflections. And teaching portfolios are often produced for authorities—program directors, certification boards, and hiring committees. We argue that we cannot assume teachers can construct a lasting "teaching self" in a teaching portfolio. Instead, a teaching self is fashioned through the teacher's resistance to and negotiation of the discourses about scholarship that connect and collide in the portfolio context. We hope that our discussion encourages further research into the implications for instructors of Michel Foucault's (1982) idea that the self is never fashioned in a lasting, unified way but is refashioned repeatedly in the discursive tensions within which the individual acts. Such exploration would seem to have significance for a conception of the teaching portfolio not only as a record of development and achievement but also as a site of rhetorical negotiation and struggle, for teachers and for all of the individuals involved in the discourses that operate there.

2

Looping and Linking Heuristics for Teacher Portfolio Development

Julie Robinson, Lisa Cahill, and
Rochelle Rodrigo Blanchard

In her introduction to an edited collection on teaching portfolios, Nona Lyons (1998) traces the development and use of teaching portfolios back to the 1980s and posits that credentialing and assessment were not the only uses to which teaching portfolios were put. She argues that teaching portfolios can be regarded in multiple ways: "as a credential, as a set of assumptions about teaching and learning, and as making possible a powerful, personal reflective learning experience" (4).

With the rise in teaching portfolio development and usage, exciting possibilities emerge because teachers can reflect on their professional activities. However, tensions can also arise because outside audiences may not view teaching portfolios unconditionally. Even when classroom practices, theories informing those practices, and beliefs as well as philosophies about teaching and learning expose the creative potential that exists for teachers, tensions still arise from contextually imposed requirements on the teacher and the teaching portfolio. Many of these externally evolved tensions arise from institutions that have adopted and "monolithically imposed" (Roemer, Schultz, and Durst 1991, 475) teaching portfolio standards that generate commodified, prepackaged teaching assessment "kits" (Schell 1996, 180). Many of these "kits" include some type of an evaluative assignment that contains a list of required objects, artifacts, or reflections for the portfolio.

These sorts of institutionalized standards often dictate lists that promote an uncritical collection concept system, rather than a critically self-aware portfolio system that emphasizes the contextualized nature of teaching (Brookfield 1995, Campbell et al. 1997, Hamp-Lyons and Condon 1993, Lyons 1998, Shulman 1998, Snyder et al. 1998, Yancey 1992). A portfolio system that emphasizes the contextualized nature of teaching returns freedom of choice to portfolio makers, enabling them to decide what types of material to include, what organizational structure works best, and what presentation format is most suitable. Without this freedom to develop form based on function, teachers may find themselves compelled or obliged to include materials that do not adequately communicate their teaching identities, philosophies, and performances. Thinking about the function of teaching portfolios "as revealing a set of assumptions about teaching and learning, ones shaped by a portfolio maker" (Lyons 1998, 4) enables teachers to reclaim some of the promise held by teaching portfolios.

Teaching portfolios can function as documents that make teaching identities visible (for example, through teaching philosophies and letters of recommendation) and show evidence of teaching performances (for example, through lesson plans, assignments, and activities) to different audiences who have a variety of motives for reading the portfolios depending on their degree of power and influence. But by representing teaching identities and performances through portfolio documents, they become accessible *and* assessable. To take full advantage of the promise of teaching portfolios—to become critically reflective—teachers need the time and space to customize their teaching portfolios into communication tools that contextualize their teaching performances for themselves and their readers. In recognizing these tensions, teachers are better equipped to identify, negotiate, and make use of different obstacles that arise when teaching portfolios are private (reflective) and public (rhetorical). To do this, portfolio development processes should address the shifting professional needs and demands experienced by a teacher during different points in her or his career. In this way the portfolio starts as a means for self-discovery with an eye toward an eventual public and rhetorical presentation.

Rather than offer strict advice about how to "best" construct a teaching portfolio, we provide heuristics for teachers interested in negotiating the reflective and rhetorical elements involved in teaching portfolio construction. Throughout these heuristics we advocate a "loop-and-link" approach for constructing the portfolio. Looping means that the portfolio author revisits questions, reimagines the answers, and reperforms what it means to be a teacher. Linking involves the act of connecting belief systems to practices (the reflective to the rhetorical), beliefs and practices to the theoretical, and processes to the product. In particular, we provide strategies for developing a highly personalized working teaching portfolio while including a foundation for how to adapt that working draft to meet specialized rhetorical situations.

We envision the looping and linking stages as occurring across a three-stage continuum: the first stage begins with recording and examining classroom practices and experiences; the second stage involves contextualizing those notes and reflections by linking them to beliefs, theories, and practices; and the third stage loops and links materials in order to construct a teaching identity and to communicate examples of teaching performances to multiple audiences in various rhetorical situations.

Linking to One's Self

Searching for how a belief system manifests itself in teacherly practices makes the construction of a teaching portfolio critically self-aware. George Hillocks, Jr. (1995) describes this practice when he writes that reflective writing teachers "continually reexamine assumptions, theories, and practical implications at every stage from developing knowledge for practice, to planning, interactive teaching, and evaluation" (xviii). Julie Robinson and Tracy Singer (1999) explain that by "looking into a personal set of values, histories, beliefs, and responsibilities teachers form philosophies in sync with their psyches" (3). They argue further that it is these philosophies that move classroom practice out of the domain of tacit knowledge and into a more metacognitive awareness. Robinson and Singer also argue that personal definitions of *knowledge, success, intelligence,* and *literacy* provide the framework for developing systems for classroom management, text/material selection, instructional methods, and assessment (4). As teachers consider how values develop and reemerge over time, their classroom practices, artifacts, and classroom observations reveal the philosophies that went into their selection in the first place. This ongoing practice of reflection keeps teachers connected to personally defined pedagogical values while also making theoretical adjustments as necessitated by new contexts, new courses, and new knowledge. This attention to reflection works well as a starting point from which to build a working teaching portfolio or a "pre-portfolio" because it asks teachers to return to their personal belief systems as a starting point.

Presumably, all teachers have bits and pieces of what "feels right" in the classroom (and portfolio) because they already have ideas in place about what knowledge, success, intelligence, and literacy mean to them personally. Answers to the questions, "What is important to me as a teacher?" and "How do I make my teaching values consistent in my classroom?" manifest themselves in classroom practice. For this initial loop in the process, research involves bringing the values that individual teachers hold dear to the surface so that they can scrutinize practice. For example, "knowledge" may take the form of an entry in a teaching journal describing a student who posed a well-articulated question in a large group discussion. The acknowledgement of this act in the journal says *something* about how the teacher views the term *knowledge*. The next step is to consider what that *something* about *knowledge* means. In-depth reflection requires a further teasing out, which enables teachers to reloop through their ideas. The choice—to look at students and record some thoughts about them—moves teachers away from uncritically labeling themselves as "social constructivists," or uncritically aligning themselves with another theoretical term, and moves them towards theory construction advocated by Pierre Bourdieu (1990)—determining theory through practice.

Looping to One's Self: A Heuristic

1. Keep an informal teaching journal of activities and moments (successes and failures) in your teaching practices.

2. Have the journal reflect (loop) back on itself and other entries. One easy way to accomplish this is to record thoughts on the right side of each page and keep the left side of each page available for moments when you return to comment on previous entries.

3. Consider ways you define *knowledge, literacy, success, intelligence, learning,* and other pedagogically-related terms. Do those definitions manifest themselves in your teaching? How do you know? Is your assessment method consistent with how you view definitions of literacy? What about text selection? How do you manage your classroom instruction? What does small group work or direct instruction say about your definitions of intelligence or success?

Linking to Contexts

Marilyn Cochran-Smith and Susan L. Lytle (1993) describe reflection as the process of documenting teaching, which involves teachers redefining "their own relationships to knowledge about teaching and learning, [as] they reconstruct their classrooms and begin to offer different invitations to their students to learn and know" (101). After exploring *knowledge,* for instance, teachers can locate sources of support by building a network of information from people who view knowledge in the same way. This stage in pre-portfolio development is much like the ancient rhetoricians' concept of *copia*—gathering resources for foundational support.

This is the time when teachers hash it out with themselves about whether they are more comfortable with the "making meaning" camp popularized by Ann Berthoff (1981) or with a definition of knowledge consistent with Stephen North's (1987) "marketplace" of "multiple and competing" forms of knowledge. Much like Peter Elbow's (1973) metaphor of cooking, teachers working through this process should consider these definitions as "bubbling up" after looking at their own practices (48). Collecting support in this manner links teachers to outside scholarly contexts and enables reexamination (and possibly rearticulation) of personal beliefs as contextualized definitions.

For many teachers, this stage in the process of documenting teaching becomes the proverbial filing cabinet full of articles that "make sense." Included in this cabinet may be empowerment rationales like the ones featured in the

May 1998 edition of *English Education* where English studies educators mapped out explanations describing the thoughts that went into the formation of their practices. Another possible artifact in this copia could be a never-mailed letter to the editor standing up to a critic who published antieducation sentiments in a local newspaper. Teachers interested in gathering foundational support through community building may also work beyond the confines of a filing cabinet by forming educational action committees, book clubs, or writing circles. All these practices are ways for teachers to get to know themselves better in the context of teaching. None of these acts are necessarily produced for public scrutiny; think of copia more as an extended teaching journal that responds to the question, "How can teachers compose effective teaching identities that are both helpful to themselves and that account for the specific needs of different disciplines and circumstances?"

Decisions about the kinds of materials that best reflect ideas regarding theory, pedagogy, and practices provide a springboard for curricular conversations between networks of teachers, students, administrators, and community members. These situational exigencies call certain teaching identities into action by discovering when, why, and how a teacher suppresses or enacts a particular theory, pedagogy, or practice. Articulating these discoveries provides material for teaching portfolios in the filing cabinet stage.

To continue reexamining core sets of teaching beliefs, teachers should consider the situated contexts in which their classroom roles and methods intersect with students, disciplinary ideologies, and institutional or departmental missions. Mary Rose O'Reilly (1998) contends that "most of the odd things I do in the classroom have evolved from the struggle all of us go through between the norms of our discipline and the demands of who we are" (32). Continually reflecting on outside influences can help teachers learn how to balance the multiple roles and identities that must be adopted in order to meet the demands of different contexts. Becoming aware "of the norms of our discipline" is a critical step in the struggle between self-reflection and rhetorical awareness. Self-reflection reveals what is important to the individual teacher while rhetorical awareness makes an understanding of contextualized identities and practices possible. Simultaneously working through theoretical, pedagogical, and practical influences forges conscious connections between all three while also enabling recognition of any inconsistencies.

The places from which theoretical, pedagogical, and practical influences can spring serve as a starting point for reflecting upon the beliefs and experiences responsible for shaping teaching in contexts. Specific mentors, theorists, colleagues, places, courses, texts, lessons, and experiences may have contributed to teaching theories and practices. This next set of heuristics is designed to orient teachers to the contexts in which they work while acknowledging how these contexts impact teaching performances and identities in positive and/or negative ways.

Linking to Contexts: Gathering Copia

1. Think about how theories derived from your discipline, education, reading, and life experiences influence your work. For example, consider how you rethink a particular concept after dialoging with colleagues.

2. Copy and store files of articles from your ongoing reading of professional articles and books that appear to match your personal and professional philosophies. Keep track of quotes and passages that speak to you as a teacher.

3. Consider how past and present course/content, methodology, instructional training, interactions with students, administration, and social/cultural environments influence your teaching practices. For example, consider how grant money devoted to enhancing student achievement affects issues related to collaborative learning with a diverse student population.

4. Remember to loop back to your teaching journal from time to time to brainstorm ways your reading influences your work. Keep track of favorite scholars, instructional ideas, and philosophers who provide foundational support for your professional practices.

Looping and Linking Through the Rhetorical

Although it is quite a feat to produce a teaching philosophy and portfolio that is personally satisfying, it is quite another feat to make the leap to a rhetorically sound portfolio. While moving between a reflective and rhetorical portfolio can cause tension, it can also have a productive effect. For example, some institutional standards call for portfolio development that is both reflective and rhetorical, such as the Teacher Education Program at the University of California at Santa Barbara (UCSB). UCSB requires that M.Ed. students construct both a credential portfolio and an M.Ed. portfolio (Snyder et al. 1998, 129). By assigning two portfolios, UCSB implicitly recognizes the tension between the need for an individualized, reflective portfolio and an institutionalized, rhetorical (audience-centered) portfolio. Although both contexts ask teachers to construct portfolios for specific, official audiences, the M.Ed. portfolio becomes more personal to the teachers, since they are asked to "pursue their passion" during its construction (Snyder et al. 1998, 129). This personal-to-professional development continuum allows a teacher to embrace, rather than reject, the tensions in constructing reflective and rhetorical portfolios. This continuum idea also exists in the Elementary/Early Childhood Department at California University of Pennsylvania (CUP). The teachers within the CUP education program keep a personal portfolio characterized by an "ongoing systematic collection of selected work in courses and evidence of community activities," that helps "form a framework for self-assessment and goal setting" (Campbell et al. 1997, 3). They are also expected to construct a presentation portfolio by selecting specific artifacts that reflect the needs and interests of intended audience members.

Because of the issues at stake in the construction, solicitation, and reading of portfolios, it is important for teachers to consider larger issues surrounding portfolio development when linked to presentation. The inclusion or exclusion of particular materials, ideas, lessons, examples, and theories in the teaching philosophy *and* in the supporting sections of the portfolio is often dependent upon both specific audiences and their intentions. Before making a portfolio public, teachers need to consider questions about the portfolio's audience, purpose, and potential effect on the reader(s).

Working through the exigencies created by transforming a pre-portfolio (copia) into a rhetorical portfolio can help teachers note and examine the pressures that emerge between the reflective work that may be personally useful to them and the rhetorical space/reward for documenting teaching. Because rhetorical portfolios link documentation to multiple audiences, teachers must remain flexible enough to accommodate change, including large- or small-scale revisions, deletions, and additions without feeling compelled to misrepresent their teaching identities, practices, and philosophies. Rhetorical portfolio construction must represent—and critically engage—the contexts in which teachers operate, keeping in mind departmental, institutional, and disciplinary goals.

Linking and Looping Through the Rhetorical

1. *Audience:* Who is the audience for/of your portfolio? Why are they your *target* audience? Do you get to choose the audiences who will read your portfolio? How conscious are you of your audience(s)? Who else is your audience "reading"?

2. *Purpose:* What kinds of disclosures are you offering in/through your portfolio and to whom? What kinds of compromises are you comfortable making? Why does your audience have an interest in your teaching?

3. *Effect:* How do portfolio documents influence your professional identity? What kind of assessment and evaluation will your portfolio facilitate? What types of feedback (if any) will your audience provide you? How will that feedback affect you professionally? What is at stake for your audience if your identities and philosophies appear different from their own?

Looping Back

Can teaching portfolios live up to the promise of more accurately representing teacher knowledge, ability, and practice? Kathleen Blake Yancey (1992) asserts that learning portfolios enable students to become agents of change because portfolios open up, for both students and their teachers, "new ways to learn to write; new ways to think about the teaching of writing; new ways to read and understand our students, ourselves, and our curricula; and new ways to describe and then report on what we find" (vii). We believe that Yancey's claim is directly transferable to teaching portfolios. Teaching portfolios can be constructed for mutual benefit between multiple audiences when their authors take into consideration reflective and rhetorical elements of teaching. Reflection is both self-discovery *and* self-construction; therefore, teachers constructing portfolios need to recognize that the heuristics needed for such discovery and construction can be both rigorous and exhilarating. However, administrators and community members, such as students, parents, and state legislators, also need to join teachers in recognizing just how much work it takes to first critically and comfortably reflect on one's teaching and to then represent that work in a portfolio.

The promise of teaching portfolios will continue to go unrealized until teachers are offered more support for the development of their teaching portfolios. Portfolio development can be better supported by placing more value on the time it realistically takes to gather materials, reflect on those materials, and then organize them into a rhetorical document. To support this potentially time-intensive process, schools or departments could survey teachers to learn whether they would like in-service portfolio workshops. Schools or departments could also provide time and space during the week for small groups of teachers to meet to discuss their portfolio progress. Additionally, portfolios can facilitate productive dialogues between teachers and community members who can learn more from the teacher about his or her classroom decisions and practices. In this way, rather than only using teaching portfolios as evaluative tools or for accountability, the portfolios can be viewed as a mechanism for dialogue.

With this freedom in teaching portfolio development, teachers, who have consciously chosen to work beyond prescribed portfolio "kits," can begin to recognize that they (should) have more control over the construction and presentation of their identities. They do not have to allow rhetorical considerations of audience and purpose to overpower the critically reflective construction of their teaching identities. With this acceptance and recognition, we work toward the promise portfolio advocates see as being possible.

3

Thinking and Writing Ethnographically for Annual Reviews and Promotion and Tenure Portfolios

Sarah Robbins

As I write this essay in the fall of 2001, the portfolio I prepared to be the cornerstone of an application for promotion to full professor is slowly moving up a hierarchy of evaluating committees at Kennesaw State University (KSU). While I, of course, cannot predict the end result of this professional assessment process, I have—thankfully—already received highly affirming endorsement letters from the English department promotion and tenure committee and from my chair. In the coming months, I will be receiving additional evaluation letters from a college-level committee, my dean, the university committee, the vice president for academic affairs, the president, and the state university system's central administration. Despite the consistent responses I have already garnered from my department's "p and t" committee and chair, I approached the preparation of my portfolio with some trepidation. Others currently involved in this high-stakes process have not, in fact, been as fortunate as I have, so far. Perhaps one cause of the divergent evaluations emerging between some department-level committees and their respective department chairs is the fact that we are working at a university in transition.

Given both the special challenges of preparing documentation on teaching at an institution with a shifting identity, and the larger context of a growing, nationwide emphasis on assessing teaching at the university level, I have sought help with this important professional task in my training as a teacher researcher. Specifically, I have developed strategies for documenting my teaching for annual review and for the promotion portfolio by using ethnographic data-gathering and analysis techniques similar to those I employ when studying my own or others' instruction for research on the culture of classroom communities. In this essay, I describe the changing institutional context where I work and the ethnographic strategies I've developed for assembling, interpreting, and presenting information about my teaching in this context.

One goal of this essay is to argue that using ethnographic strategies for representing our teaching affords us some control over the evaluation of our teaching at a time when more and more stakeholders are demanding accountability. Toward that end, I will show that we in composition and literacy studies are especially well-equipped to learn about ourselves as educators by gathering open-ended information about our own teaching and interpreting it inductively, even though we must be strategic about how to present what we find.

Balancing Teaching, Scholarship, and Service at an Evolving Institution

Just under forty years old, KSU is located in the northern suburbs of Atlanta, an area of persistent population (and associated economic) growth over all the years of the university's existence. Local lore says that the site for the university was chosen by political leaders who pointed to a state map's dotted lines, which were indicating the future trajectory of Interstate 75, and who predicted that positioning a junior college near Marietta at a highway exit would support economic development in a region still dominated, in the early 1960s, by its rural heritage. Whether or not this folktale is true, it communicates a core element in the institution's culture from that founding moment to today—close connections between KSU and the community whose burgeoning educational needs it serves. Said another way, from its early days as a junior college, through its expansion to a four-year college, to its current position as a public, regional university, KSU has been, first and foremost, a teaching institution emphasizing applied learning and community connections. Along those lines, the university's official mission statement declares, "Effective teaching and learning are central institutional priorities. Service and research that strengthen teaching and address the public's interests are important supportive priorities."[1]

Intertwining this focus on teaching with a commitment to community-based growth, KSU has exploded from a relatively intimate learning environment of about 3,000 students in its junior college days to around 13,000 today. As its student population and campus facilities have expanded, so too have its academic offerings. In particular, with the emergence of graduate programs like the two for which I teach—a Master's in Professional Writing and a Master's in Education—conceptions of faculty "work" have changed. Longtime faculty members often say that expectations for performance have shifted fairly

---

1. (For the full text of the mission statement, see *http://www.kennesaw.edu/about/mission.shtml.*)

dramatically, from instructional success being the clear hallmark of faculty excellence to a far more complex (and some would argue demanding) vision of faculty labor at KSU.

Questions about the relative weight of scholarship versus teaching have become especially challenging as KSU's commitment to graduate education and its effort to enhance its academic reputation have grown. In particular, for those faculty who have been assigned "graduate teaching status," scholarship has shifted from a category that could be designated by individuals as their "second area" in evaluative importance (after teaching) to being a category that *must* be judged, after teaching but before service, as the measure for advancement. As the faculty handbook notes, "KSU expects the full professor who has graduate faculty status to be more active and productive in the area of Scholarship & Creative Activity than is expected of full professors without such. . . . Graduate faculty typically do not have the option to emphasize Professional Service over Scholarship & Creative Activity as a primary area of emphasis. . . ."[2] At the same time, though, guidelines for promotion and tenure still signal a primary emphasis on teaching. Thus, the criteria for promotion to full professor address teaching issues:

> Full professors are expected to continue to be highly effective and highly accomplished in teaching, supervision, and mentoring by experimenting with, revising, updating, and improving their techniques for working with students and others as effective facilitators of learning. Highly effective professors should continue to make strong contributions and take leadership roles in curricular and instructional development, evaluation, or reform.[3]

Because teaching is the major evaluative criterion for faculty, KSU is a place where documenting teaching is a high-stakes enterprise, especially given the mixed audiences that may evaluate a candidate's material. A typical promotion and tenure committee at department, college, and university levels includes both longtime faculty whose 4/4 loads may encourage them to view teaching at least partially in quantitative terms—how many students served, how many sections taught, how many different courses developed since the last review. Serving on the same committee will be administrators who are trying to "move" the faculty—especially the relatively new hires who are sometimes more likely to be teaching in graduate programs—to a view of pedagogy linked more self-consciously with scholarship. Fortunately, administrators and faculty with all types of responsibilities have worked together to create promotion and tenure guidelines recognizing the range of duties and contexts applicable to individual KSU faculty, as well as suggestions for how faculty can prepare the required portfolio elements. Those suggestions invite productive synthesis of teaching,

---

2. See *http://www.kennesaw.edu/academicaffairs/tenure/hdbkt&p.htm#PromFullProf.*
3. See *http://www.kennesaw.edu/academicaffairs/tenure/hdbkt&p.htm#PromFullProf.*

scholarship, and service.[4] Despite such support (including workshops and a listserv for candidates), however, the notable emphasis evaluators place on teaching excellence during the review process places a great deal of pressure on the teaching philosophy statement and the selection of supporting materials. In light of that pressure, as I looked ahead to applying for promotion to full professor this year, I developed a strategy for using the other regular (and more frequent) occasion for evaluation of my teaching—the annual department-level review—as a step that would prepare me for the "big" portfolio that lay ahead. Before characterizing that annual research-and-reporting process, I outline my conceptual framework for analyzing my teaching ethnographically.

Thinking Ethnographically About My Teaching

Logistically, developing an ethnographic stance for documenting my teaching is dependent on two basic processes: creating informal field notes and gathering artifacts throughout my teaching year. My "field notes" are informal because, like all teachers, I have very little time to write about my instructional decision-making on a regular basis. But I do jot comments in the margins of handouts (those that "work" and those that don't). I write down the score distributions for major tests and papers. And I sometimes print out emails responding to student queries or comments, as a way of keeping track of those exchanges. In addition, after grading student work, I may print out a copy of the assignment and make notes about how to change it, or I'll save both the original and a revised version. My artifacts are material examples of my teaching life. I keep syllabi and major handouts, for instance. I also save representative copies of student work (after asking permission) and statistical records of student learning (for example, printouts recording the number of hits on a course Website or the number of student entries on a computer bulletin board).

Gathering materials to assemble a portrait of my teaching is only an initial step, of course. Wendy Bishop (1999) presents "four core features" of ethnography that I have used to organize and interpret data about my teaching:

> First, it is inductive rather than deductive. Second, the data are open to many interpretations and are not collected in a closed set of analytical categories. Third, investigation is intensive on a small number, even as small as one, of cases. And fourth, the analysis is an explicit interpretation of the meanings of

4. See *http://www.kennesaw.edu/academicaffairs/tenure/philosop.htm.* Along those lines, for a thoughtful discussion of the inadequacy of the traditional triumvirate used to evaluate faculty work—scholarship, teaching, and service—see Slevin. Slevin's efforts to show how faculty can "lead an integrated and significant intellectual life" by doing work that is along a "border-line" or enacting a "mix" of the traditional categories has been helpful to my thinking. For instance, Slevin describes one hypothetical faculty member whose teaching includes directing a WAC program, developing new courses, advising and recruiting students, and leading summer programs as well as instructing in traditional courses (297).

language and human actions. When statistical analyses are used, they play a
subordinate role (6).

As outlined above, I save artifacts in folders using categories such as students'
solicited and unsolicited communications,[5] sample "strong" and "weak" student
products, class notes, workshop agendas, reports to grant agencies,[6] and students' evaluations. I gather this data not course-by-course but in the categories
outlined above, because I'm not seeking to do a case study of a particular class
but rather a study of my teaching in all its forms. At year's end, I review the material (often in rather thick piles) to identify patterns, ask questions, and form
tentative observations about changes and continuities in my teaching. Along
the way, as Bishop suggests, I keep in mind that "the data are open to many
interpretations," and that they are "not collected in a closed set of analytical
categories." Thus, I don't look for particular abstract, predetermined traits of
my teaching in these materials. Rather, I watch for new "patterns" to emerge.
For example, when reviewing my material recently, I discovered a recurring
goal of mentoring professional writing with advanced students.

I can afford to make my investigation intensive, because I typically teach
fewer sections per term than my colleagues, spending most of my time administering grant-funded programs for which my teaching is more community-
oriented and less tied to course sections. In any event, as Bishop indicates, I
devote my analysis to "explicit interpretation of the meanings of language and
human actions." That is, I study my data to see what patterns of language *in* and
about my teaching emerge, and how my students and I behave in the community
of our classroom. When I use statistical information, I do so to check inferences
that have emerged from more qualitative interpretations. For instance, one year
I noticed that several students in one course wrote in their open-ended final
evaluations about assignments being excessive, with a few even saying they
were "tired" or "discouraged" by the end of the term. Checking my gradebook,
I saw that average scores for projects at the close of the semester were, indeed, somewhat lower than scores on early assignments—the reverse of what

---

5. An example of a "solicited" communication would be the midpoint reflections I generally ask
   students to write in a course—comments about changes they would like to see in the class, as
   well as things that seem to be going well. "Unsolicited" communications would be the types
   of letters and emails students send me without any prompting—sometimes during a course, but
   more often afterward.
6. Several of my classes in recent years have been grant-related or even grant-supported. For example, while directing a National Endowment for the Humanities project on studying community
   cultures, I taught an honors seminar using the themes and instructional strategies our project
   team had developed collaboratively during a summer institute. In this case, looking for matches
   and mismatches between my report to our funder about the content of our program (as framed
   by the proposal for funding) and the instruction I provided in my own course was clearly in
   order. Similarly, I've taught individual courses supported with grant funds from the University of
   Georgia system (for teaching with technology) and my own institution (for "faculty incentives"
   to improve pedagogy). In those cases I would want to juxtapose the language of the original
   proposal with artifacts such as assignments and student work.

usually happens in my courses. I realized I must have worn my students out! This pattern led to conversations with colleagues who taught in the same program (an M.Ed. for middle school teachers), reading their syllabi, and revising my assignments.

Ownership, Authorship, and Argument Preparation: Using the Annual Review as a Pre-Portfolio Process

Major occasions for faculty evaluation at KSU raise issues of ownership and purpose for representing teaching. For instance, annual review is officially constructed as an occasion when teaching is evaluated by me and my chair in order to describe progress and set goals for growth in the following year. Given the institutional primacy of teaching, KSU asks its faculty members to write a narrative philosophy and teaching report every year, including both reflective self-assessment and proposed teaching goals for the upcoming year. In official documents such as the faculty handbook, the annual teaching narrative and supporting documentation are constructed as formative moments, helping to enhance a faculty member's professional development. Yet, because the chair's annual review letter (written in response to the narrative report) becomes a part of the official record that goes forward in a candidate's portfolio at promotion and tenure review points, faculty must attend to the larger narrative that is emerging about their teaching over several years, and to the ways in which those representations will feed into summative evaluations at promotion and tenure time. Thus, while presented as formative, I would maintain that the annual review narrative of teaching is always already summative and belongs to multiple evaluators more than to the faculty member (see Leverenz in this volume).

For two reasons, then, I have tried to make each of my annual teaching narratives ethnographic texts. First of all, using ethnographic principles and practices to gather data for my narrative each year grounds the (pseudo)formative process in a scholarly tradition that matches my view of the classroom as a unique culture—a community with its own value systems and social practices. Second, presenting my annual teaching narrative by using ethnographic techniques allows me to report in a hybrid informant/researcher voice whose rhetorical authority is hard to resist.

Establishing an authoritative stance for talking about my teaching is especially important. Besides preparing for the promotion process, annual review also directly affects my salary. In addition to analyzing our service contributions and scholarly achievements, we are required to submit course syllabi and student evaluations for the previous year. We are also required to produce a philosophy statement and narrative about our teaching, in which we must address any concerns relevant to the student evaluations and other data (for example, grading patterns different from the department norm). This blend of structure (required elements) and open-endedness (choice about how to frame our teaching philosophy and how to present our narrative) makes the writing we do for annual reviews complicated rhetorically, because we have only partial control over what we can present, but substantial control over how we present it.

On one level, the teaching narratives are self-evaluations drawing on ethnographic research of my teaching. I generate my inquiry questions, study my practice reflectively over the review period, then make my analysis the centerpiece of my teaching narrative.[7] Such a strategy allows me to discuss openly some of the "failures" I experience in my teaching by framing them within the context of teacher research, so that even those shortcomings can demonstrate good teaching as I "perform" self-critique. For instance, in the annual teaching narrative I turned in for the year 2000, I looked ahead to fall 2001, when I would be team-teaching a course on women's work in the nineteenth century. I knew the course would invite students to consider how images (for example, on advertising cards, in newspaper photographs) shaped social conceptions of women's place in the 1800s and would include having students create their own Web pages to analyze such images via cultural context from history and literature. With this challenge on the horizon, I made one of my teaching-inquiry questions an investigation of how effectively our two-person teaching team could balance having students interpret visual culture through new technologies. The report on this class in *next* year's teaching narrative will be a condensed teacher-research analysis, considering the implications of what I learned. Along with framing one or two teacher-research questions each year, however, I also examine my practice from a completely open-ended stance, including observing interactions in my classroom and monitoring exchanges with students.

One crucial element in this process involves seeing the materials that cross my desk as cultural artifacts of teaching, not just ephemera. For example, it was only when I read through a six-month pile of students' unsolicited notes one year that I recognized a new pattern in my mentoring.[8] Increasingly, my students and former students were writing for publication—in journals, in newspaper editorials, in newsletters for their professional organizations. Their communications suggested that I had taught them how to navigate the publishing waters. This pattern confirmed a match between something I was already trying to value explicitly in classes—the idea that writing for publication is a worthwhile goal—and what I sometimes call my "interpersonal curriculum," the teaching that I do with students outside of class time (in conferences, at events). More specifically, what I noticed in the written exchanges was a tendency for students to construct me as a coach for professional development beyond the official

7. For helpful suggestions on researching teaching, see Hubbard and Power (1993), *The Art of Classroom Inquiry.*
8. See Moore (2000), who argues that tenure and promotion committees need to develop formal categories for describing and valuing student mentoring.

curriculum. Their notes depicted me as somebody who wanted to know if they sent out a piece they had originally composed for class; as somebody who would read a revision before it was submitted; and also as somebody who had helped them see connections between the content of the course and other discourse communities where they wanted to become vested participants. For instance, one woman wrote about how she had gained a new job after publishing an essay in a magazine, and she credited me with helping her to write "toward" this new professional identity. Another wrote to thank me for an open-ended project assignment that let her try out a new genre she had later mastered with more practice, leading to a promotion at her current job. Once I noticed this pattern, I could think about its implications for my teaching—how I might support this "writing toward" process more directly; how I might help students learn to mentor each other as well as count on me; what I might learn by tracking where my students were publishing. Asking myself these questions eventually gave me the idea for a new course—one focused explicitly for teachers affiliated with our National Writing Project site on publishing in professional journals.

Overall, noticing patterns of value and practice in the many artifacts of my teaching gives me increased ownership over my professional work. Instead of merely reacting to the "results" of impersonal evaluation forms, this process allows me to interpret my classroom records for my own professional growth, even though it also serves to measure my progress in others' eyes. To assess how well I am (or am not) carrying out a coherent philosophy, I reread the statement I wrote the previous year and assess whether the data I've collected affirms its major components. Sometimes, this analysis prompts me to adjust my philosophy—to describe how it has evolved. Other times, the comparison encourages me to change some practices in the next year so that I can better enact my philosophy. At the same time, this analysis helps me to create a rhetorical framework for (re)presenting my teaching to others—my chair and committees evaluating me—by highlighting the strongest matches I can find between philosophy and practice.

Balancing the necessity to sing my own praises in these annual reviews with the ethnographer's aim of being trustworthy is sometimes challenging. But researchers reporting on their observations of others also bring biases to the task. My goal, then, is not to efface my own perspective and goals but to be attentive to how my own stance is shaping my interpretations. "Ethnographers today worry less about trying to see things as they are and more on explaining how their enterprise grew from a careful reading and is presented in a certain way" (Bishop 150). When writing about my own teaching for professional review, then, I use ethnographic techniques to ensure that my interpretations are as trustworthy as possible. And, as I would when writing about someone else's teaching—i.e., when doing ethnographic research where I am purportedly more observer than participant—I concentrate on making my position in the culture clear, on highlighting the thinking processes I used to draw certain conclusions about my teaching, and on emphasizing connections between those conclusions and the often contradictory data that I have gathered. Said another way, I try to write in an honest authorial voice, acknowledging that I was the person "in charge" of guiding the culture of my classroom, that I am also the person interpreting how that community functioned, but that I am analyzing both of those processes with as much attention to the *ethics of representation* as I can muster.

Below is an example of how I try to balance those contingencies when writing about the aspects of my teaching that have been less than perfect. In this case, the open-ended evaluations students had written at the end of a graduate course in professional writing split over one particular issue—whether or not I made a good decision, midway through the course, when I began using written questions and small-group discussions around reading assignments that some students were finding very difficult:

> A notable number of those enrolled were taking their first... graduate course—i.e., had not even had the core course yet. Thus, they lacked such "basics" as a common vocabulary of terms associated with the study of writing in our graduate program—e.g., "discourse community," "audience," "genre".... I made a variety of adjustments along the way to support the insecure students—e.g., answering their requests for help with their reading (which some of them termed "very hard to understand") by preparing questions to guide their analysis for longer or more complex texts; planning more small-group discussion activities for class so that the tentative students wouldn't feel drowned out by the especially vocal and confident members of the class, as they occasionally had been at first when I used more whole-class discussion. Interestingly, these very moves to (in educationese) "scaffold" the less capable students occasionally left the most talented class members feeling a bit constrained—as a couple of voices in the evaluations indicated. I sense that, on balance, the trade-off was a necessary one in this case, but I am glad that our shift to... an every-term offering of the [core] course... will make the extreme diversity in preparation levels of class members that was evident in this group less likely in future courses.

In this case, as I often do, I started with the data of student evaluations, read that data in light of other contextual material (for example, input I had received from struggling students during the course), checked other sources of information for corroboration (that is, the online student records that verified how many students had been taking their first course in the program), and positioned my interpretation within an argument I was already developing as the rhetorical hook for my narrative that year—that all my teaching activities had been aimed at ensuring every student a genuine opportunity for success. This interpretation certainly left room for me to adjust my practices in future courses (for example, to use more conferencing with insecure students and less scaffolding during class time), but it also prevented the voices from a small number of informants in the student evaluations, complaining about only one aspect of an otherwise successful course, from undermining my own (or my chair's) sense that the class had been a good one.

Representing Teaching in the Promotion Portfolio

As I write *this* narrative, I have recently completed my promotion portfolio over four years of teaching. Complicating this representation was the fact that much of my teaching has actually been directed outward from the university. I teach a range of English department courses, graduate and undergraduate, including classes in American literature and women's literature as well as courses for two Master's programs, one in professional writing and one in education. But an increasing percentage of my typical semester workload involves running grant-funded programs—creating and evaluating workshops, administering budgets, collaborating with teachers working on research teams, recruiting participants, and mentoring other teachers who are participants in ongoing projects. I teach at institutes for K–12 educators during the summer, through the National Writing Project and other funding sources such as the National Endowment for the Humanities, and I teach professional development programs during the year. Perhaps half of my teaching does not involve traditional courses.

Because of strict limits on the size of promotion portfolios at KSU, I could present only a brief, simplified story of my teaching in these diverse venues. Thus, representations of my work in university courses—the type of teaching most colleagues would find easiest to understand—took on great importance. Knowing this would be the case, in the years just before I went up for promotion, I tried to imagine all my syllabi as having multiple audiences—my students, but also my upcoming evaluators. Thus detailed course syllabi became one key component in my portfolio (see Website examples).

Even more important, however, was my teaching philosophy statement. Before drafting it, I reread all my annual teaching narratives since my last promotion, looking for traits I could highlight that were apparent in courses as well as in the grants-based teaching: I then checked for signs of these same core traits in other bodies of evidence (i.e., the observations and artifacts described above), and I considered which traits could effectively illuminate connections integrating my teaching with scholarship and service. To write my introductory narrative for the whole portfolio and the particular section describing my teaching, I not only drew on past annual reviews, but also upon unexpected discoveries in the teaching artifacts that I had been saving since my last promotion portfolio. Finally, I reread the university's mission statement. When I realized that its emphasis on "community" connections coincided with one of the major teaching themes that had emerged inductively from my analysis of past annual review narratives and other artifacts, I chose that theme as the "hook" for my portfolio's overarching philosophy statement and narrative description of my teaching (see Website for full text).

Having written and revised my narrative, I realized this documentation process made visible some ideas about my teaching that would have remained vague and unfocused otherwise. By making the day-to-day work of teaching less familiar and more worthy of contextualized cultural analysis, taking an ethnographic approach toward representing my teaching has helped make me more aware of the reasons behind my instructional choices and the related implications for future professional growth that can be derived from reflective critique. Although I do not yet know how all the readers in the evaluative hierarchy of KSU's promotion process will respond to the portfolio, I do know that these ethnographic research and writing processes will be guiding my teaching in the months and years to come.

4

Constructed Confessions: Creating a Teaching Self in the Job Search Portfolio

Peggy O'Neill

Reflection is one of the defining features of a portfolio, one that transforms a collection of various texts into a portfolio according to scholars such as Kathleen Blake Yancey (1998) and Peter Seldin (1997). As Yancey explains, reflection constitutes "the processes by which we know what we have accomplished and by which we articulate accomplishment" and "the products of those processes" (1998, 6). Although Yancey is referring specifically to reflection associated with the writing classroom, it holds true for teaching portfolios constructed beyond the classroom context, which I discovered while creating a teaching portfolio for my initial job search out of graduate school.

While reflection is an integral part of a portfolio, it is not an innocent or ideologically free activity. In fact, in my own scholarship (dissertation, conference presentations, and essays) I have begun to see the reflective writing of student writers akin to the Christian rite of confession as Foucault (1990) analyzes it:

> The confession is a ritual discourse in which the speaking subject is also the subject of the statement: it is also a ritual that unfolds within a power relationship, for one does not confess without the presence (or virtual presence) of a partner who is not simply the interlocutor but the authority who requires the confession, prescribes and appreciates it, and intervenes in order to judge, punish, forgive, console, and reconcile; a ritual in which the truth is corroborated by the obstacles and resistances it has had to surmount in order to be formulated; and finally, a ritual in which the expression alone, independently of its external consequences, produces intrinsic modifications in the person

who articulates it: it exonerates, redeems, and purifies him; it unburdens him
of his wrongs, liberates him, and promises him salvation. (62)

Although I wasn't looking for salvation, I was in search of my own little piece
of heaven—a tenure-track job. As part of the "ritual" of the job search, I was
required to document my teaching, constructing a teaching "self" through discourse. Search committees, the authorities requiring the discourse, have the
power to judge candidates based on such application materials. As I worked
on my portfolio, I was well aware of the high stakes. I attempted to balance
my desire to create a persuasive portfolio that would contribute to securing a
job interview or campus visit with the obligation I felt to present an accurate
account of my teaching and myself as a teacher. I began the teaching portfolio
reluctantly because I have never been able to keep a teaching journal (or any
kind of journal), although I like writing and see the value of written reflection
(using it often in my classroom). In other words, I wasn't comfortable in the
position that the portfolio created for me—a willing participant in constructing
a text that exposed my teaching for others to judge. Because of my reluctance
to create a portfolio and the context for which I was creating it, I did not expect
to experience any beneficial consequences. In the words of Foucault, I didn't
expect that "the expression alone, independently of its external consequences"
would produce "intrinsic modifications" in me. Now, looking back from the
relative security of a tenure-track job, I realize that in the process of creating
the portfolio, I learned about myself, my values, and how I wanted to be perceived as I moved from being a graduate student to an assistant professor. In
this essay, I focus on the principles and processes I used to construct a "teaching
self" through the portfolio's products.

Processes

Despite waiting until a few months before the October *MLA Job List* to work
on my application materials, I had long been preparing for the job search. An
English graduate student cannot avoid the doom and gloom forecasts about the
academic job market. As I entered a Ph.D. program fresh from the front lines
of public school teaching, I got the message loud and clear: start preparing for
the job search now. Early on I began gathering material about academic job
hunting and continued to prepare and work toward the dreaded job search by
participating in local workshops organized by experienced graduate students.
Although most of the information focused on standard job search materials
such as the curriculum vitae and letters of recommendation, discussions about
documenting teaching became more common. I went to several workshops on
teaching portfolios, including one given by a graduate student in our program
on how he constructed his teaching portfolio for his successful job hunt.

Because I had decided early on that teaching was a primary focus of my
scholarship and professional identity, the teaching portfolio became a central

document. Initially I saw the portfolio as a way to distinguish myself from other candidates; but as I created it, I found that it required me to articulate the theories and practices I valued, forcing me to reflect on my teaching as I struggled to represent myself. What I first saw as a savvy marketing tool became a site for professional development. In hindsight, I realize that my experience is not unusual (Seldin 1997; Tietel, Ricci, and Coogan 1998).

Like all portfolios, teaching portfolios are diverse, diffuse, and undefined. As I prepared for the job market, I concentrated on what I already knew about portfolios from using them to teach and assess writing in my classrooms, what my fellow graduate students shared from their experiences, and advice gleaned from workshops and presentations. As Chris Anson and Randall Woodland (1997) have stated, not all teaching portfolios are the same. As with any text, audience, purpose, and context are significant factors in the construction of a portfolio. Most experts and experienced faculty agree that a portfolio designed for the job search is not the same as one used for ongoing professional development or even tenure and promotion. Carrie Leverenz and Amy Goodburn (1998) argue that "helping new TAs become effective and thoughtful teachers" is different from "professionalizing graduate students for the academic job market" (13). Teaching portfolios compiled for the purpose of self-reflection and improvement are different from those created for self-promotion: "[I]n our experiences as readers of job candidate recruitment and merit files, the value of the teaching portfolio is measured not in terms of growth or development but in the degree to which teachers represent themselves as successful" (1998, 13). But even portfolios intended for self-reflection and improvement need to consider audience. Laurel Black (1997) discovered that a teaching portfolio can make the teacher vulnerable depending on the audience(s): some portfolios are not safe places for learning from or reflecting on practice. My goal, then, in creating the portfolio was to present myself as a professional and successful teacher to search committees. To achieve my goal, I relied on the portfolio process that I used with students: collaboration, collection, selection, and reflection—activities that both helped me to create a polished product and allowed me to grow as a teacher.

Collaboration

Although most literature on portfolios (whether for writing or teaching) identifies the portfolio as a collaborative enterprise, this can be difficult to realize when composing a job search portfolio. The job search is, after all, competitive and one can make oneself vulnerable by exposing materials for review. As I prepared my teaching portfolio, the most valuable part of the process was working with my colleagues Cindy and Jane, two fellow graduate students also preparing for the job market. We discussed audience issues in depth. We knew that the portfolio could hurt our chances depending on how it constructed us: we wanted to represent ourselves as successful while still being accurate. Cindy and Jane helped me articulate my strengths and refine my language, but also kept me honest. Because they knew me, they helped me avoid self-promotion and remain faithful to what I valued and how I taught. I tried to sound knowledge-able and committed, but I didn't want to sound too theoretical or use too much jargon. I also didn't want to sound like I had all the answers, as if anybody who did things differently was wrong. My readers would have lots of materials to review in a short time, so I needed to be concise and limit the portfolio contents.

Cindy, Jane, and I were able to help each other by discussing important issues such as content and presentation, by providing feedback and revision suggestions, and by listening to each others' questions and anxieties. Although we were applying to many of the same jobs, we were able to be positive and supportive instead of competitive. Every aspect of my teaching portfolio—and theirs, too—was discussed, reviewed, and revised by us. We shared our resource materials, our primary documents, our drafts. We talked about how we wanted to "sound" to our readers, and we tried to read each others' work as we anticipated it would be read by our intended audiences. Admittedly, every once in a while we might have felt awkward or insecure about how we compared to each other, but since we had different specialties and different requirements for a job, we were able to remain encouraging. Working with Jane and Cindy not only helped me create a better product, but also made the process more worthwhile because they pushed me to reflect on my teaching and find ways to accurately represent it. For example, in workshopping a draft of my teaching philosophy, Jane and Cindy prodded me to articulate more clearly why I try to make students independent writers and what I mean by that. By working with supportive and knowledgeable colleagues, I was able to explore and reflect on my teaching; from reading and commenting on their materials, I was able to learn new things about teaching, the representation of teaching, and the reading of portfolios.

Collection

Collecting materials was one of the easier steps since I had been doing it long before I decided on including a portfolio as part of my application materials. I already had syllabi, handouts, student work, and course evaluations from all the courses I had taught as a graduate student as well as materials I developed for workshops. Gathering them was quick and easy, although the accumulated pile seemed a little daunting. I also collected some materials from the teaching I had done as a public school language arts teacher before entering my doctoral pro-gram because that experience had been crucial in my development as a teacher.

Selection

Selecting materials, which occurred over several weeks of reviewing, reflecting, and talking with Cindy and Jane, was more difficult. I decided to use primary documents from my teaching as well as secondary texts to help shape the way these primary documents would be read. The primary materials focused on two different writing classes, "Intermediate Composition" and "Advanced Composition," showing them in some detail because they illustrated a range of my teaching abilities (see the Website). For each course I included the syllabus, assignments, handouts, and student evaluations. I also included a syllabus from a graduate seminar, "Teaching College Writing," that I had cotaught twice; an assignment that linked college students with high school seniors; and two evaluations from my secondary teaching experience. To contextualize these documents, I wrote several texts including an introduction to each course and a teaching philosophy.

Each document was chosen to represent something about my teaching or to showcase what I could do. I wanted readers to get a sense of my range of teaching experiences and interests, so I tried to choose documents that did not reiterate something I included elsewhere but that were consistent in terms of theory and practice. For example, I included a Listserv Report assignment for the Advanced Comp. class because it illustrated how I incorporated technology into my classroom. For the Intermediate Comp. course, I included detailed guidelines for the portfolio students assembled because they illustrated many of the theories I discussed in my teaching philosophy.

Of course, discussions and decisions about what documents to include in the portfolio automatically incorporated debates about what to exclude. I eliminated student work for many reasons. First, I was afraid that grades and responses wouldn't travel well because student writing is so highly context dependent. I thought that search committees might contain members of the "grade police" who would think I was too easy, too lax with grammar, or who would not be able to accurately evaluate my responses. Conversely, some committee members might think I was too tough, too stringent, or insensitive. Student writing and responses to it should be interpreted through the context that informs them, but my readers would not necessarily understand my context (in spite of my attempts to explain it in the portfolio) and would be reading through theirs. Secondly, I didn't have permission to include students' work and didn't want to compromise my ethical position, especially in application materials. I also excluded faculty evaluations of my college teaching because these faculty had written me letters of reference; I did not want the portfolio to be repetitive of other documents. Including too much might overwhelm readers and result in critical information being overlooked.

Reflection

Reflection, as I knew from using portfolios in my classroom, was not an isolated step in the process but rather integrated throughout. Cindy, Jane, and I talked about our past and our future teaching, our experiences as graduate students, and our hopes as professionals. We helped each other make connections among what we had done, what we wanted to do, and how our portfolio might help us achieve these goals. I also spent time alone reflecting as I reviewed course materials, made selections, and drafted documents. And of course, I spent time talking with my partner about individual and group reflections, processing things even more (and I know Cindy and Jane did the same with their partners). Reflection then permeated all parts of the portfolio process, as we moved back and forth and through the different aspects of making decisions, revising work, rewriting.

Through this process, I started to realize that deciding on the contents and the presentation of the materials really involved figuring out who I was as a teacher and how I wanted to present myself to others who would judge and evaluate me. Would they find me acceptable, or would they send me to the reject pile? Although the portfolio showcased my success as a teacher, the processes—especially the collaboration and reflection that it demanded—were rewarding for me as a teacher. The false starts, failed experiments, and revisions that I actually experienced in constructing the portfolio—and in the classroom as a teacher—fostered growth and development even though they were not visible in the polished and professional portfolio products.

Products

The texts I wrote for the portfolio benefited from the processes in which Cindy, Jane, and I participated. Creating my portfolio demanded that I articulate in clear, concise language a teaching self or selves. As a veteran teacher, I had a strong sense of myself as a teacher, but I had not had to convey that to an unknown, unseen audience. The dilemma, of course, is to try to present oneself accurately while attempting to appeal to the reader, who might or might not share one's values, approaches, or commitment to teaching. After all, we all wanted a job, but we didn't necessarily want just any job. If we misrepresented ourselves, we might end up in a place that did not support our theories and pedagogies, a place that would not value our teaching. Worse yet, we might get overlooked by a college or university that could be a perfect fit.

The products were also critical in illustrating our writing abilities. We wanted to be sure that the committees knew we could write well, not just teach well. Armed with an understanding of portfolios and with supportive colleagues—not to mention the anxieties that accompany the academic job search—I created my portfolio. The final version contained several reflective documents: an introduction, a philosophy of teaching, narratives for each course, and summaries of the student evaluations. (See the Website.)

Introduction

The introduction, which I wrote last, was a way to guide my readers, to help them see the merit of certain documents and to show the reasoning that went into the construction of the portfolio: "Although I have a wide range of teaching experience, I highlight my most recent. . . . Intermediate Composition is a course that I have not only taught frequently but also have been involved in preparing new instructors to teach." I thought about the instructions I gave my students for writing their portfolio introductions—make it reader-friendly, be specific, highlight what you want me to notice, show what you know. I knew that the introduction could get my readers interested in my portfolio or turn them off, and I wanted to establish my authority, my ethos, while providing some important information. The opening line states, "As a former secondary English teacher, I have logged many classroom hours" because I wanted to be sure the committee knew that I was an experienced teacher and that teaching public school was an important aspect of my identity. I had first learned about teaching writing, student-centered activities, and classroom management as a seventh-grade language arts teacher and was very proud of that experience. However, I also knew that many English professors did not value this kind of experience. For example, after reviewing my job search materials, one of my graduate professors had told me that I looked too "educationy" for most English departments and recommended that I downplay my experience and interest in education. I appreciated her concern, but I didn't want to work in a place that devalued public school teaching. I realized as I worked through the portfolio that my experiences in public school were major influences in how I defined myself as a teacher and why I pursued my doctorate in composition and rhetoric. Besides, I thought that my public school teaching might distinguish me from other candidates and make me appealing for positions that included teacher preparation (and it did).

Philosophy of Teaching

In my teaching philosophy, I stressed the diverse influences that formed my approach to teaching: my experiences as a writer, student public school teacher, college writing teacher, and teacher-educator while emphasizing my positive attitude about students and my commitment to student-centered teaching. Touching on strategies and approaches that are central to my teaching, such as rhetorical principles, reflection, and portfolios, I described writing as a meaning-making activity. I highlighted how issues of assessment influenced my teaching, hoping that readers would realize that my research—writing assessment theory and practice—was connected to my classroom practice. I wanted my readers—my potential colleagues—to see my teacherly self as informed, open, and student-centered.

Narratives

For each course in my portfolio, I wrote a two-page narrative that explained my goals, how the course progressed, and how students responded. I included specific vignettes and anecdotes about students highlighting the positive, such as this from my Intermediate Comp. course narrative: "For example, one student, an army veteran and father of two small children, investigated the childcare facilities on campus and tried to find a viable solution. Although his paper wasn't successful in terms of changing the situation, he discovered how complex the subject was . . ." What I did not include were comments on the quality of his paper, which was mediocre at best. For the Advanced Comp. course, I focused on the "new challenges" this course presented to me, such as teaching an upper-level course in the computer classroom during a five-week summer session.

Each narrative ended with a section entitled "Evaluation." In retrospect, this paragraph does not evaluate the classes or my performances so much as present my sense of the classes and the student evaluations. I do not dwell on missteps or the students who fell through the cracks but spotlight my success, admittedly falling into the self-promotion game that Leverenz and Goodburn critique. As a job candidate I felt too vulnerable to include the thoughts and questions that, as a teacher, I actually had. But just because these reflections do not show up in my narrative, doesn't mean I wasn't reflective or that I didn't benefit from them. In fact, much of the discussion in our portfolio group centered around teaching activities and our thoughts about them. So, for example, I noted some of the difficulties in my Advanced Comp. course, but I was still positive: "My feelings about this class were mixed: the students were engaged, they did the work, attended all the classes, and seemed genuinely interested in learning. . . . However, because of the compressed time frame, I felt—and they expressed—frustration in trying to fulfill the writing requirements, specifically research and revision." I also noted that we had had trouble with the computer equipment, which added to our frustrations. What I didn't detail was how much the technological difficulties hampered the course goals or how outdated the equipment was. My goal in the evaluation section of the narrative was to acknowledge that classrooms don't always go as planned but that I could adapt and still get the work done when the circumstances weren't ideal. Again, Cindy's and Jane's feedback helped me strike the right balance as they anticipated potential readings and interpretations, and contributed to my understanding of my classroom and the job market. I felt that I was also preparing for the interview process because we would often be responding to each others' questions about our teaching and what we were trying to communicate through our materials.

Student Evaluations

Although the majority of this section consisted of the quantitative summaries of student ratings and the discursive comments for each course, I also included a brief paragraph to explain the evaluation process at my institution and how I viewed it. Again, discussions with Cindy and Jane were critical as we explored questions such as, "Should I respond to the students' evaluations?" and "How should the discursive comments be presented?" In the final version, the paragraphs for each class seem merely informative, rather than reflective; but, lots of reflection went into deciding what to write and how to present the student evaluations.

While I received many positive responses to my portfolio on the job circuit, I am not sure how much it contributed to the success I experienced as a job candidate. However, the benefits of the portfolio, especially through the meetings with Cindy and Jane, made the process of creating it successful for me because I learned more about teaching and myself as a teacher, created a polished portfolio, learned more about job search issues, and felt more prepared to talk about myself and my professional activities.

Conclusions

For me, the purpose of the teaching portfolio was to showcase my success as a teacher. Leverenz and Goodburn seem critical of this aspect of teaching portfolios as they distinguish "between self-reflection and self-promotion" (13). Although I appreciate the distinction they make between a successful teacher and a teacher who represents herself as a successful teacher, I don't think that the high stakes and competitive nature of the job hunt allow for any other approach. Besides, self-reflection and self-promotion are not mutually exclusive: one *can* be reflective and focus on growth and development while promoting oneself. As Seldin explains, "The very process of creating the collection of materials which comprise the portfolio stimulates professors to reflect on what has worked in a particular class, what has not, and what might be done to improve the quality of their instruction" (26). Maybe Leverenz's and Goodburn's distinction is important for training new TAs, but I was not a new teacher when I started working on my portfolio. Moreover, I believe a successful teacher is interested in growth and professional development; and I wanted my portfolio to show that I not only valued reflection but also saw myself as always in process. According to Lee Shulman (1998), "What is declared worth documenting, worth reflecting on, what is deemed to be portfolio-worthy, is a theoretical act" (24). While Shulman isn't referring specifically to a portfolio used for a job search, his reasoning fits with my experiences. In other words, regardless of the ultimate purpose of the portfolio—or the final portfolio product—the processes used to create it demand reflection and theoretical engagement, which are necessary for growth and development.

Working on this essay, reviewing my portfolio, and the process I went through in creating it has provided me with another venue for reflection and professional growth. It also has made me think about representations and constructions of the self through discourse. As Foucault explains about the confession, in the portfolio I was both the speaking subject and the object of that discourse. The portfolio required me to explain, in the words of Kathleen Blake Yancey, "both of the self and about the self" to an outside audience (71). But, by collaborating with my colleagues throughout the construction of the "confession," I was able to avoid some of the anxiety associated with the job search.

My entire portfolio, then, was an act of reflection prepared for an outside audience, one that would judge me and the self I constructed through discourse.

I deliberately use the singular self, although I am aware of the postmodern critique of it. As James Berlin explains (1994) in a piece that specifically links portfolios to the postmodern, "Each of us is heterogeneously made up of competing discourses—of conflicted and contradictory scripts—that make our consciousness anything but unified, coherent, and autonomous" (62). In fact, Berlin, Yancey, and others celebrate the portfolio for allowing writers to present their multiple, situated selves. As I think about and reread my portfolio, I realize that I purposely worked to present myself as a unified, coherent—maybe even autonomous—self (much like Foucault's discussion). That doesn't mean I did not experience the fragmentation Berlin notes, or that I wasn't aware of the situatedness of my position, just that I worked to present my*self,* not *selves.* In the process of creating the portfolio, I worked collaboratively to construct a teaching identity, one that can never be me, but is always already a representation, a construction. I specifically worked to create a consistent voice in my documents—both primary and secondary. As Lester Faigley (1992) explains, for all our theorizing about the postmodern, there has been "a preservation of the belief that the student writer is a rational, autonomous writer" (225). I would extend Faigley's analysis to all kinds of writers, especially those writing in high-stakes assessments, and believe me, the job search is a high-stakes assessment.

Portfolios, like all texts, are designed to achieve certain goals or demonstrate certain competencies. Sophisticated rhetoricians attempt to anticipate readers' response and manipulate the text so that it has the intended effect. How am I trying to present myself in a portfolio used for my growth and development as a teacher, especially if others such as colleagues and professors may have access to it? How does this compare to a teaching portfolio used for a job search (or tenure and promotion)? Do we assume that logs and notes are more "authentic" than polished narratives or teaching philosophies? Are these assumptions justified? Accurate? I don't really have answers to all these questions, but I continue to think about them as I use portfolios in my classrooms with my students, work on my tenure and promotion file, and read candidates' job search materials. Discussing both the processes and products of teaching portfolios is one way to resist easy generalizations or simplistic readings of them, and as I found out, one way to keep making them sites for reflection and growth.

Acknowledgments: Thanks to my portfolio collaborators at the University of Louisville, Cindy Moore and Jane Mathison Fife, for contributing to my portfolio process. We have continued our collaboration as they read and responded to drafts of this essay as well as through various other projects.

5

Teaching Statements and Teaching Selves

Ruth M. Mirtz

I had been teaching for five years before someone asked me to write a coherent statement about why I wanted to teach. It was a shock. To comply with the request, I haltingly wrote about how I wanted to make the world a better place by educating young people. Truthfully, I was still immersed in the how, what, when, and where of teaching writing, not even ready to think about the "why" of teaching writing. Moreover, I was afraid to say what I might really think: that I taught writing because I needed a job, because I did not think I could do anything else, and because some days teaching writing was really fun.

Now, fifteen years later, I've written teaching statements for a wide variety of occasions: job applications, teaching award applications, departmental annual reviews, and promotion and tenure portfolios. I no longer feel like I have to mouth idealistic phrases in order to write a teaching statement. Still, some of the same worries surface when I sit down to write yet another teaching statement: the inadequacy of my preparation, the multiplicity of my motives, the sometimes embarrassing reality of my teaching, and an aversion to boasting of my successes. Although teaching statements always sound simple ("describe your teaching and highlight your successes"), I often find myself wrestling with writing them.

The teaching statement or teaching philosophy is never just a statement or declaration. Rather, it is a teacher's chance to synthesize theory and practice, to highlight successes, to argue for specific methods, and to educate the many audiences who will read it. In most cases, the teaching statement is part of a collection of written texts designed to give a fair and context-rich accounting of the teacher's work—the document that frames an entire collection of materials (for example, statistics on student evaluations, peer observations, syllabi, and letters from outside evaluators). Moreover, terms such as "compact self-appraisal

43

statement," "candidate's evidence on teaching," and "reflective essay" reveal the wide range of expectations that a teaching statement might need to address. A "teaching philosophy," for example, is frequently expected to feature theories that inform a teacher's practices and a description of the practices themselves, often while also attempting to persuade readers about the validity of such knowledge and practices. This range of terms reflects the variety of purposes, audiences, genres, and contexts for teaching statements and points to their complex rhetorical situation. Compounding the complexity even further is the issue of self-representation—the challenge of making public what is often private, making reflective what is generally automatic, and representing as static what is generally in flux and transitional. This chapter explores the rhetorical challenges inherent in writing teaching statements, especially issues of self-representation, and offers some strategies for producing more effective documents.

Exploring Audience Expectations for the Teaching Self

Because the contexts surrounding teaching statements differ, it seems sensible to approach the task of composing such documents by studying the specific purposes and audiences for the statement. Almost immediately, then, writers of teaching statements will confront tensions that result from the competing interests of a formative, personally valuable written presentation of teaching and a statement that can reach outside audiences. Because, as teachers, we tend to see students as the primary audience for our teaching (writing documents that students read with a view toward acting on the assignments described therein), it can be difficult to anticipate the expectations of a nonstudent audience. If we discuss our individual teaching experiences on a regular basis, we tend to do so with close colleagues who are sympathetic and share our interests in teaching. We might even keep teaching journals that provide a space for reflecting on teaching. For all these audiences, we can assume connections that we may not make explicit and draw tentative or provisional conclusions.

However, other audiences (the promotion committee, the awards panel, the search committee) and the purposes that bring these audiences together place different demands on us as teachers. Ellen Strenski (1994) describes these readers' expectations and the "responsibility" such expectations construct for the writer:

> It is the writing instructor's opportunity and challenge, but it is also his or her responsibility, to begin the review process by making the best case possible for reappointment, promotion, or whatever. If a writing instructor cannot write such a letter, either because he or she is not aware of, and therefore can't explain or justify, pedagogical principles, or because he or she lacks adequate powers of written expression, then the instructor should not be reappointed or promoted. (70)

Interestingly, Strenski implies that the problem of disagreement among reviewers can be resolved by a well-written teaching statement. Strenski is absolutely correct, of course, when she asserts that teacher evaluation must start with self-evaluation, but she too quickly concludes that conflicts regarding the varieties of teaching methods and course content in an English department can be solved by writerly skill.

Strenski's faith in the power of well-written statements may be accurate in those cases where candidates know their readers well, have had opportunities to hear readers' concerns about particular pedagogies, and have some sense of the kind of evidence that readers find compelling. Yet, in my experience, most English departments do not always agree on criteria for excellent teaching, much less criteria for acceptable teaching. Added to these departmental conflicts (or silences) are the complicated expectations of audience members beyond the department—college promotion committee members, for example, who may have no experience in teaching writing. These audiences rarely specify their criteria or the value they place, for instance, on experimenting with different pedagogical approaches (or the relative weight they assign narrative accounts of classrooms in considering evidence of effective teaching). Moreover, even when criteria are made available, there is often no accounting for that criteria or no indication of the basis for agreement on the specified criteria. Too often, such audiences expect to see teaching presented as matters of performance and knowledge of one's field. In this view, a teacher should be getting better at performing the same material in relatively unchanging classrooms.

This view of the teaching self does not square with the continual growth and change I see in myself as a teacher or with the productive possibilities for the flux caused by real engagement with any number of outside influences. Precisely *because* I stay abreast of current, changing thought in my field, for example, I stay interested in teaching. Moreover, the fact that I see teaching as support for learning (rather than performance) places my teaching self at odds with some audience members' expectations. Giving a clear and complete description of myself as a teacher means choosing between describing myself in ways that seem true to my understanding of good teaching or describing myself as someone I do not fully recognize (for example, the super-teacher who solves all my students' problems).

Some scholars have recently addressed this tension by proposing a difference between identity and roles. Deborah P. Britzman (1994) writes that our roles as teachers and our identities as teachers are not the same thing, despite our constant striving to make them cohere (54). She explains that roles are outward manifestations in action and can be assigned and reassigned; identities react against roles as well as construct them and take into account knowledge-making structures and social negotiations (54). While the separation of self into differentiated roles threatens to leave us dis-integrated and fractured, it is a short-term strategy that might be turned to good purpose. Teaching roles divide, but they also organize and categorize complex activities. In Elizabeth Rankin's

(1994) study of new teachers, for example, the language of roles allows these teachers to compare cultural definitions of particular roles:

> They're not sure they want to be teachers, given the way our culture sometimes defines that role. Teachers are lecturers, disciplinarians, grammarians, authority figures. They would rather be friends, foster parents, coaches, priests, or therapists—all roles that they see more positively than the teacher role, all roles that they can see themselves performing in some way. (119)

To address the tension between the flexibility we may value in ourselves as teachers and the expectation of fixed or stable commitments that many audiences demand in teaching statements, we can focus on the parts of our teaching that are most often present. Even though most teachers frequently change their methods, emphases, and assignments, there is usually something—a concept or an attitude, at the least—that endures. For example, I have always used small group collaboration in my teaching but over the years I have changed the way I use small groups in my classes. I know from experience and from composition theory that thoughtful texts do not come from writing in a vacuum—that is, writers need readers. I could describe this concept within a teaching statement, incorporate supporting composition theory, and give one example from my teaching. But notice the progression in this line of composing—I did not start from a concern for audience. Rather, I started from thinking about why I teach the way I do.

In the end, it is easy to understand why we struggle with teaching statements in high-stakes moments: representing ourselves as teachers feels like whittling down the self to something unitary, essential, or always generally true about ourselves for unknown audiences (however wise and thoughtful many of those audience members are). Britzman reminds us, however, that our teaching statements are not illusions, but constructions, socially formed and informed. Although referring to new teachers, Britzman's work is useful for describing how all teachers move from experience to reflection to critical statement: "[D]ecentering unitary notions of the teacher while helping them move beyond the meanings that posit the role as synonymous with identity can permit newly arrived student teachers the spaces to reflect upon the persons they are becoming and thus critically elaborate the traces of their own narratives" (62). Conflicting roles create tensions within our identity-forming representations that are not going to "resolve" or sort themselves out. Thus, preparation or prewriting for teaching statements needs to include attention to writing into, around, and out of these conflicts. Moreover, some of my struggles to compose teaching statements become less threatening when I remember that teaching and writing require linguistic structure-making. Ann E. Berthoff (1990) reminds us that the power of language resides not only in its indicative function but also in its "power to represent our interpretations of experience. . . . No thinking—no composing—could happen if we had no means of stabilizing images of what we have seen, of recalling them as forms to think about and to think *with*" (35).

Through this lens, teaching statements can be conceived as forms to "think about" and "think with" as we consider our teaching lives.

Analyzing Teaching Statements

In this section I examine four of my teaching statements (included in full on the Website) for the following high-stakes occasions: an annual department review for merit raises, a teaching award application, a tenure and promotion file, and a job application portfolio. While the concerns of the audiences for these statements were somewhat identifiable, they also ranged widely enough to be unpredictable. Taken together, these statements show how I worked—both productively and unproductively—with the tensions that emerged in the conflicts between my needs as a teacher-writer and my audiences' needs as evaluators. Thus, they should not be taken as models, but as interesting cases of a teacher-writer at work.

Annual Review

For an annual evaluation, I organized my teaching statement around three kinds of changes: improvements to methods I had always used in the past, experiments with teaching methods or classroom structures that were new to me (teaching in a computer classroom), and recent insights from teaching new teachers (TAs). I tried to write to the department as a whole. For instance, because I knew the department had discussed making courses less proprietary and more connected to the English major as a whole, I described my development of courses in terms of the larger curriculum and other faculty's course goals, mentioning specifically that I "read other faculty syllabi and talk[ed] to the faculty who [were] teaching the course to find out what they [had been] doing. . . ."

The context for this statement is no doubt recognizable to many writing teachers: a department with some members who openly scorned composition, an evaluation procedure that ranked each faculty member on a single scale without any written criteria for that rank ordering, and an administration that was not likely to fund the merit raises for which the entire process was conducted. What my statement ended up representing, perhaps more than anything else, was an attitude toward the evaluation process. Assuming that my teaching statement would make little difference in the outcome, I wrote what Lisa Ede and Andrea Lunsford (1996) call "unintended discursive irony" (178). For instance, I wrote that "The graduate rhetoric courses are, I believe, stronger when the rhetoric faculty agree on the general gist of what the courses are about and don't teach whatever we are most interested in at the moment." Admittedly, that was a jab at colleagues who taught graduate courses based mostly on their current research. My insertion of "I believe," unnecessary in a teaching statement, points to the fact that I was using the teaching statement as an opportunity to have a voice in department and programmatic practices.

At the same time, I was trying to write a teaching statement that accurately reflected some of the major changes I had made in my teaching as a result of moving to a new university and entering a new writing program with different goals and different students. Foregrounding these changes reflected my belief that adapting to program goals and students' needs is what makes teaching good. Some of my audience, however, certainly (mis)read this as lack of experience. (Phrases such as "trying to do a better job" and "I'm getting better at" probably contributed to this interpretation.) In retrospect, perhaps I should have described my efforts in stronger terms, leaving aside the ambiguity inherent in such verbs as "trying," and "experimenting."

By writing out of my attitude toward the evaluation process, I missed the opportunity to educate my colleagues about what I do. Richard Gebhardt (1997) describes this instructional feature of our teaching statements:

> It is easy to think of tenure review and various pretenure evaluations (year-end chair reviews, reappointment evaluations, merit-pay reviews, and the like) as one-way transactions in which personnel committees, faculty members, chairs, and deans judge the work you describe and document in various required reports. But while they are studying the report you submitted (updated CV, compact self-appraisal statement, selected course materials, recent articles, etc.) these women and men are learning things about your work and your field. (124)

While I agree with Gebhardt, it is not always easy (nor, perhaps, wise?) to trust that one's audience will agree as well. Thus, I defended (rather than educated others about) my teaching, explaining that some students were "forced to take the class in order to have or keep their teaching assistantships," and other students believed "that they already knew everything about teaching writing." In the end, readers would have been surprised to know that I found my teaching that year to be enlivening and rich. This statement suggests that I relished nothing about my teaching. My attitude toward the evaluation process overwhelmed the representation of teaching that I was trying to construct.

Teaching Award

The second teaching statement was written for a major university teaching award (which I won). The audience was a committee of faculty from across the university, and there were no specific guidelines for writing the teaching philosophy. I did have previous years' winners' portfolios to read and previous members of the committee to consult. What I wrote feels, even now, like a better and more appropriate representation of my teaching than my statement for the departmental annual review because it assumes the viewpoint of a teacher with years of experience and many successes. Interestingly, while "change" is still a theme, I locate that change in the past: "Back then, I didn't realize..." what I know now as an experienced teacher. Only two paragraphs are devoted to a specific recent revision in my thinking and practice, and that revision is described in terms of what stays the same: "One of the recent changes in my own teaching has been in what I consider the 'content' of a first-year writing course. While I still focus a great deal on the writing skills that all students need to develop, I have learned that those skills don't translate into abilities unless they are contextualized as language issues." In the context of this statement, "change" becomes an enduring (and therefore defining) feature of my teaching.

The rest of the philosophy points, as well, to what is *consistently* true of my teaching: I "take a stance," I "see myself working," I "frequently use," and "I know from my experience." I write about small group collaboration, students as learners, and my roles as fellow writer, expert writer, and observer of students. In writing about changing definitions of literacy, I write about how change outside my classroom has required me to change my teaching, rather than how I am changing in order to be a better teacher.

Writing for an audience outside of department readers not only prompted me to reconceptualize the place of change in my teaching, it prompted me to think more productively about the educational function of teaching statements. For the departmental evaluation I wrote that "I've improved greatly on the research project after teaching it, rather haphazardly, in the fall of 1994," signifying an unorganized teaching plan and offering no specifics about what I changed. However, for the teaching award I wrote: "For instance, when my first-year students work on advanced mechanical rules such as the use of semicolons, they also need to discuss how ideas connect and how brains create categories, in order for the use of a semicolon to become the meaning-making choice." I didn't expect my audience to understand which categories of thinking are required for understanding semicolons, but I was showing more specifically how writers need to know more than rules to use punctuation effectively.

Promotion and Tenure Portfolio

While I imagined a friendly and less-knowledgeable audience for the teaching award, I had to assume an even wider audience with different interests in my teaching for a third teaching statement— this one included in my promotion and tenure portfolio. Of course, most audience members were knowledgeable, supportive faculty who read tenure portfolios carefully and thoroughly. However, the audience also certainly included the same kind of cynics as the departmental evaluation as well as faculty from other disciplines facing very different pedagogical challenges. This time the statement was called "evidence on teaching," indicating that the statement represented proof or verification of something in one's teaching. "Evidence on teaching" was described in written guidelines for tenure as including "a statement by the candidate describing the candidate's teaching." This requirement was followed by a paragraph regarding how to report student evaluations. While a reader might surmise, thus, that student evaluations were much more important evidence for the tenure and promotion portfolio, the statement of evidence was still the only place where the candidate could highlight or explain his or her teaching.

My "evidence on teaching" is a revision of the statement for the teaching award; in fact, some paragraphs are exactly the same, although some awkward sentences are improved. Instead of starting with a story about change and ending with a look toward future changes in my teaching, however, the statement for promotion and tenure starts with a summary of my teaching philosophy and ends with an even broader view of my educational philosophy. The story of my becoming a teacher is shortened from five sentences to two. I also eliminated discipline-specific terms, changing "meaning-making" to "meaningful act." The word "critical" is added, denoting (in some circles) rigor and abstract thinking. Some of the third-person material is omitted in the tenure statement in order to focus the statement solely on my teaching. The overall effect is one of making the statement even more declarative and assertive, more like the result of a career full of good teaching rather than teaching as a work-in-progress.

In the tenure statement my theme of change further mutated to a statement about the purposes I see for teaching philosophies: "I feel that the best teaching philosophy is a working document, subject to consistent change as a teacher (including myself) tries to improve her teaching." In my award statement, the concept is a personal one: "My teaching philosophy will, of course, continue to evolve . . . ." Again, looking back, I see both sentences as scaffolding left over from earlier drafts where I was trying to state my purpose. However, nothing unsuccessful or "haphazard" appears in the award or tenure statement, in part because I had begun—through the use of these forms—to think of myself as a teacher who changes purposefully (not constantly).

Job Application Portfolio

In a teaching statement composed as part of a job application, I again had to anticipate readers' desires for a fixed, assessable teaching identity. First, I moved discussions of how my practices have evolved to the very last paragraph. In the form of a conclusion, the story of my changes as a teacher is again contextualized in terms of emphasizing current expertise (instead of learning from failure). As a result of my experience on search committees, I realized that job application files are read quickly, so I chose to put one main idea (student-centered classrooms) in the first paragraph. I wanted to construct a teaching self via a few fundamental philosophies that take different forms at different times: "My philosophy of teaching centers around student learning; that is, I focus on what I can do to help my students learn and how I can structure a classroom as a place of discovery and engagement for all students." I followed up with a teaching self divided into roles:

> I see my role in the classroom as multi-faceted: as the facilitator, I set the tone
> for the class and arrange the classroom environment so that all students are
> encouraged and challenged; as the expert writer, I engage students in complex
> issues about reading and writing and refuse to allow easy answers or quick-
> fix solutions to problems; as the evaluator, I use formative feedback to push
> students to do their best work.

Some of these sentences feel like statements specifically written to minimize
potential conflict. For instance, I placed my continuing experiments with computers in the writing classroom within a sentence that would be difficult to
debate: "While I have not yet found a fully satisfying hypothesis for critical
literacy which accounts for computer-networked communication, internet research, and student Websites, I feel that area of study holds a great deal of
promise for improving our instruction." After all, who in my audience would
have found a "fully satisfying hypothesis for critical literacy"? I also hedged the
question of just what kind of improvements I see happening in my instruction.
The strong possibility that my job portfolio would reach a department where
some members feel computer classrooms are a waste of time and money made
it necessary to both emphasize and qualify my philosophy of technology.

Viewing all four statements as a process, I see them moving to more nuanced understandings of audience, from tentativeness to directness, and from
descriptions of specific classroom activities to descriptions of teaching philosophies. These movements are the result of progressive efforts at documenting
my teaching—"thinking with and thinking about" (in Berthoff's terms) my
teaching via the form of teaching statements—reencountering the competing
interests of various audiences, and revising and (re)presenting my teaching for
different purposes and different audiences.

Moving Past Reflection and Analysis

We seldom receive any feedback on our teaching statements. Even though we
might rank them as "successful" based on jobs offered, merit raises received,
awards given, and tenure granted, they may not be "unsuccessful" simply because those tangible rewards were not forthcoming. Teaching statements are
part of a larger picture of our teaching provided in concert with student evaluations, letters of recommendations, and past experiences. Thus, we never know
the exact impact of the teaching statement within that larger presentation of our
teaching self. Lack of feedback, along with uncertain audiences, ambiguous definitions, and mixed purposes require the writer to negotiate the problems and
possibilities in teaching statements. Some strategies already mentioned in this
essay are: (1) Explore what keeps one teaching in order to find documentable

and meaningful "successes" in one's teaching; and (2) Represent the multiple selves and flexibility of our teaching as roles we negotiate, foreground or background. The following questions can guide prewriting toward the teaching statement:

- When and why did I decide to become a teacher?
- How does my teaching relate to my administration, service, scholarship, and community work?
- What principles serve as the foundation of my teaching? Where did those principles come from?
- What kind of teacher am I? What kinds of teacher have I been in the past?
- When and where do I consciously focus on a single goal or purpose for what I do?
- Who will read this statement and what do they value in teaching?
- Where do my methods conflict with my ideals? How do I manage the conflict?
- What sacrifices do I make to keep my teaching coherent?
- Where do I disagree with colleagues (in department, school, discipline) and why?
- How does my teaching differ from (and share commonalities with) teaching in other departments and disciplines?
- What do I admire in other people's teaching? What do other people say they admire in my teaching?
- What do existing documents or guidelines for the teaching statement seem to say "between the lines" about teaching?

As this essay makes clear, any writing that emerges from these questions will need to be revised for the wider audiences entailed in high-stakes documentation of teaching. Essentially, reflective exploring can be a first step, but the second step must follow: changing tentative possibilities into declarative statements. In other words, reflective teaching must include exploring the forms and structures of the teaching statement itself.

However, reflective teaching does not happen in a vacuum or at the desk of a teacher revising a teaching statement. Our evaluators share with us this task of exploring the forms and structures for representing teaching. In fact, it may not be possible to see our teaching statements as transformative occasions without the critical involvement of all the readers of our statements. A significant audience for our teaching statements may be those readers who have little inclination to understand our focus on student texts and processes, or little appreciation for the range of variation possible within a category called "good teaching." In order to share these explorations and experiments and to break out of the traditional concepts, we need what Min-Zhan Lu (1999) calls "critical affirmation," whereby examining conflicts of identity and representation through writing "can initiate exchanges in which colleagues—bystanders and persons in action—could become coinvestigators of not only the problems needing to be posed but also how to go about addressing them" (192). Conversations about what constitutes good teaching—not only during high-stakes evaluation but as an ongoing part of one's work as a teacher-scholar—are crucial components of this process of critical affirmation.

6

Peer Observation as Collaborative Classroom Inquiry

Deborah Minter[1]

... [T]he guy in the glasses brings the discussion to [verb] tense. You bring this distinction back into focus. Good! But you talk about it in terms of organization (and maybe purpose). Interesting that the writer has nothing to say—how disempowering this has been for her.... You seem to get stuck in answering their questions about how to write and that becomes transference of knowledge. How do we get them to come to this understanding themselves?

> —excerpt from a peer's observation, videotaped whole-class draft workshop (from my class), spring 1990

Every year, the principle comes into my classroom for 90 minutes. He has a "multiple intelligences list" and we're evaluated for how many different intelligences we tap in 90 minutes. We're supposed to cover at least 10 in a 90-minute period.

> —excerpt from conversation with Nebraska high school English teacher, summer 2001

1. The seminar participants whose work is profiled here (many of whom generously commented on earlier drafts) enriched my thinking and this chapter immeasurably: Denise Banker, Joanna Findlay, Amanda Gailey, Rochelle Harris, Melissa Hamilton Hayes, Karen Head, Andy Jewell, Stan Johnson, Daniel Justice, Justine Courtney Reilly, Darcie Rives, Rose Rodriguez-Rabin, Mike Schueth, and John Struloeff.

Classroom observations have long been a staple of assessing teaching effec- tiveness. Like the high school English teacher quoted above, I was routinely assessed through classroom observation during my earliest years as a teaching assistant. A "mentor" assigned to me by the university would visit my compo- sition classroom once a semester, sometimes videotaping my teaching (that is, setting the camera on a tripod with me squarely in the center of the frame and only occasionally panning that small part of the room that the camera could capture from its fixed perch). We would then meet to discuss what the mentor saw as she observed my class during the taping. As a new teaching assistant in the department, I met weekly with the mentor in a small group of first-time teaching assistants. (So, our mentors would have gleaned some knowledge of our classroom goals from prior conversations with us about our classrooms.) Still, I do not remember any conversation prior to the classroom observations in which we discussed our goals for the particular class meetings being taped. Given the absence of such discussion, one might expect that I (like the high school English teacher quoted above) had a clear sense of the criteria being brought to bear on the classroom or my teaching. However, I don't remember having that kind of knowledge either. Perhaps not surprisingly then, the "de- briefings" that followed these mentors' observations left me bewildered. I knew that my teaching could be improved: I saw students' lack of engagement and I felt myself floundering with the programmatic requirement of whole-class draft workshops. After watching the videotape, my mentor encouraged me to study Socratic questioning in order to improve my performance—advice that left me feeling even further adrift.

So that same semester (spring 1990), I asked one of my peers—a graduate student whose insights on teaching composition and English studies curricula I found particularly generative—if she would be willing to watch the videotape and give me some feedback. "I could do that," I remember her saying. "What kind of feedback do you want?" Until that moment, it had never occurred to me that I might shape the observation. I had not considered, for example, the sheer range of questions one could ask about a class meeting or the range of possible purposes for observing. [See both Flannagan (1994) and Strenski (1994) for competing accounts of the usefulness of classroom observation in assessments of composition teaching.] Nor had I given any thought to how the length and frequency of observation might affect the kinds of knowledge possible through such work. Mostly, I remember fumbling, saying something about being ineffective and wanting to know what she might see as she watched the tape.

Some of what she saw is reproduced in the epigram that opens this essay, excerpted from the handwritten notes that she gave me after we met to discuss the video. Some of what I learned from that experience is reflected on that page of notes, where my own writing draws large, attention-getting brackets around her observation regarding the "transference of knowledge" and the invitation to consider how we might get students to "come to this understanding themselves."

I learned that classroom observation could animate significant ideas that I had considered theoretically via my reading and writing as a graduate student in composition and rhetoric. More importantly, I began to see peer observation as a valuable means of collaborative inquiry into teaching and learning. Whereas the first conversation with my mentor identified a shortcoming that could be ascribed to (and addressed by) me as an individual teacher, the second conversation connected my struggle as a teacher to a larger collective challenge that faces all English teachers: How do "we" enact what we believe about literacy teaching and learning?

After graduate school I took my current position, sharing responsibility for preparing graduate students to teach writing. As a part of that work, I frequently teach a graduate seminar in Composition Theory and Practice that is required of graduate teaching assistants in English during their first semester of teaching. In developing a course project requiring peer observation, I revisited the earlier tension I felt between my commitments to the productive possibilities of classroom observation and the confounding experience I initially had with mandated classroom observation. From that experience—and informed by scholarship on collaborative learning and teacher research in composition as well as education research on peer observation—I developed a series of course activities (required readings, informal writing, organizing questions, and so on) that culminated in a collaborative, classroom-based inquiry project in which peer observations of classrooms are the primary method of gathering information about literacy teaching and learning. A prior informal writing assignment (one of several assigned over the course of the semester) afforded students some initial experience at attending to and representing classrooms. At the center of this essay, however, is a critical examination of the larger and more formal "Collaborative Classroom Inquiry Project." (See the Website for texts of both assignments.) This essay explores the challenges and opportunities made available by this assignment sequence and closes by reconsidering the place of classroom observation in broader initiatives to improve and assess composition teaching.

Collaborative Meaning-Making in Peer Observation

In *Composing Critical Pedagogies,* Amy Lee (2000) offers a brief description of the kind of intellectual project—and the place of peer observation within that project—that I was hoping to foster in the graduate seminar. "When we visit one another's classrooms," she writes of her ongoing exchange with colleague Shari Stenberg, "we do so not to produce an official evaluative account of an individual teacher's 'performance,' but to represent for one another our classrooms as texts that we can read critically, with the aim of better understanding what is happening and why" (135). A crucial feature, then, of the "Collaborative Classroom Inquiry" assignment is to structure (and emphasize) peer observation as part of a larger collaborative project to gain understanding about composition classrooms (as opposed to making observation part of an evaluative project). Additional important features of this assignment correspond, broadly, to "steps" in the inquiry process. First, collaborative teams form around a shared pedagogical question, interest, or concern. Second, the group sets aside time to share course materials (including course goals), and develops together some guiding questions or lines of attention that will direct their process as observers in each others' classrooms. Third, after carrying out their observations, group members share the data they have gathered and collaboratively author a "write-up" that explores how this data informs their thinking about the question or concern that formed the basis of their inquiry. Finally, I ask participants to author individually a short reflection on their experience of the classroom inquiry project.

This highly collaborative structure and inquiry focus seemed to support students in making their teaching available to others for the purposes of critical engagement with classroom practice. Here, for example, is an opening passage from one pair's collaborative write-up in which they describe their overall project. Note that the authors represent themselves actively defining the questions that guide others' attention to their classrooms:

AJ: When [we] got together initially, we expressed concerns with our students' investment in their writing and class discussion. After talking for a bit, we decided that in order to investigate something "observable," we ought to stick to class discussion. I wrote out several concerns, including the depth of discussion in my classroom, the role I played as "authority" over that discussion, and whether or not my discussions were too "safe" to be sufficiently challenging.

AG: [His] questions articulated our shared concerns. I am a little troubled by what seems to be an invisible barrier in my classroom that keeps my students from applying our class discussions, the issues we raise about the readings, etc., to their own lives and writings. I wondered how I might get my students to become more personally involved with the issues and concerns we address in class, since there seems to be a rather large gap between the depth and vigor of their class discussions and the relatively "safe," uncontroversial material they choose to explore in their writings. In order to observe particular classroom phenomena that involves these issues, *I asked [my classmate] to consider when observing my class whether I actively involve many students in the discussion, and whether I tie the subject of class discussion into the students' own roles as writers.*

AG: *I, in turn, focused my observation questions on my role as facilitator of discussion: how many of my students actively participate? Where are their eyes while they speak (just on me or on each other)? How often did I speak as the teacher? Did I help my students challenge themselves intellectually by leading the discussion toward substantial topics?* (Emphasis added).

Individually reflecting upon his experience with this project, one of the pair represented above writes:

> Though I felt comfortable that the observation was not a critique of my teaching methods, I was pleased that I had an energized day in class, that [my classmate] could witness a "good day." This response, of course, suggests that there is always a level of critique during an observation (I think a denial of that would be naïve), but I do think that it can be pushed away, that co-inquiring can be foregrounded over co-critiquing. Proof of that, I think, is the very positive colleague relationship that this activity helped create. . . .

These excerpts suggest that the collaborative structure and the larger framework of classroom inquiry helped peer teachers experience as valuable another teacher's presence in their classrooms.

If the collaborative structure helped students to experience the value of sharing their classroom practices with one another, it also functioned to subvert the master/apprentice dynamic that can surface in other models of classroom observation—a dynamic that can (albeit inadvertently) construct a passive role for the "observed" or less experienced teacher. Researching and developing this assignment, I read several publications connected with the scholarship of teaching movement, including Larry Keig and Michael Waggoner's (1994) *Collaborative Peer Review: The Role of Faculty in Improving College Teaching*. While such texts proved to be valuable resources for thinking about classroom observation—and while Keig and Waggoner's text in particular emphasized the importance of peer evaluators and explicitly championed the use of classroom observations for the purposes of teacher development rather than evaluation—I found myself, nonetheless, troubled by its representation of classroom observation. First, the featured heuristics reinscribed the activity of teaching as an individual performance rather than locating it (as Lee and others have) within the larger intellectual and scholarly challenges specific to teaching as both a general and discipline-specific site of scholarly work. Secondly, though useful starting places for me in developing the classroom observation assignment, the available heuristics seemed to place the observed in a passive role with regard to classroom observation—a difficult position from which to actively construct and offer ideas about classrooms and particularly fraught for first-time teachers.

While at least one class member was nervous about his potential to contribute, "not because I didn't know how to do it or I thought it would be too tough, but because I'm a first-time teacher," excerpts from a single group's individual reflections show how much each person valued the contributions of the others. Denise Banker writes:

> [A] component to the collaborative work that never finds its way to paper . . . is . . . the discussions we had as a group. Karen, John and I talked at length about our teaching styles. We were each significantly surprised that each one of us taught differently. Karen managed, negotiated, and encouraged discussion

in an informal manner; I used groups with prepared questions; John used board work, questions and writing reflection. I really wish I had a tape recording of what we actually said to each other at our meetings. It would be fascinating to study it further.

A second group member, Karen Head, reflects on the collaborative dynamic this way:

> The three person dynamic really highlighted the differences in our teaching styles.... The cross-sections between us created the kind of positive tension that illuminates a shared space and creates the kind of learning moments that are most significant and memorable.

Finally, John Struloeff (the third member of the group) describes their work together as follows:

> More key than the actual observations was [sic] the discussions the three of us had. As we discussed the details of our observations, those details became starting points for extemporaneous (yet very helpful) discussion. We met three separate times, and each time the conversation could have gone on for hours (and the first meeting it did).

Models of classroom observation that relegate opportunities for meaning-making to the observer (primarily) while placing the observed in a less active role do little to engage developing teachers with their own classrooms and the challenges of teaching writing.

Among the most significant of positive outcomes regarding this assignment was the degree to which it engaged us in teaching as a site of scholarly work. As the preceding excerpts attest, students came to see this kind of observation-based inquiry as an important and productive form of research. In his efforts to articulate its significance and distinguish it from other kinds of scholarly work, one student reflected: "To talk to someone and acknowledge like theoretical stances is one thing, but to see another enacting that theory in the classroom is quite different." For many in the class, this project informed their final project for the semester in significant ways. One student—part of a group that used this project to explore the dynamics of class discussion—embarked on a reconsideration of silence and its possible meanings in classrooms for her final project. Another student—part of this same group—used his final project to research formal and informal mentoring relationships in English graduate student education and devoted a section of that final project to a discussion of his experience with this project.

This project also offered me similar opportunities. As I've suggested, the activity of developing this assignment was extremely generative for me—sharing drafts of the activity with colleagues and considering their feedback; placing more general research on the peer review of teaching and classroom observation in dialogue with examples of teacher research in composition (such as Lee) and with theories of collaborative learning such as Reagan et al. (1994) and Bruffee (1993). Not only has this activity created opportunities for active engagement with composition classrooms and contributed to a teaching culture in the graduate program, it has helped me to think in new ways about graduate education in English. Equally important and generative for my thinking, however, is considering the limits and challenges of this assignment.

First, as is true in any collaborative effort, the multivoicedness that collaboration preserves is not always generative and certainly not—as a general rule—*easily* generative for students. One student explores this issue in her individual reflection:

> After finishing the peer observation project . . ., I have begun to think about a lot of different issues. First, in relation to the project, I realize that we didn't find an answer to our question. I know we discussed this in our collaborative essay, but on a more personal level, I was quite frustrated by this. I guess I wanted to find some magic answer as to how I could change the way discussion happens in my classroom. Now, I realize there are no magic answers and because each class is so different there is no one way to make "discussion happen." Interestingly, I just finished a midterm evaluation in my class. This is something I usually do in my classes. . . . An overwhelming majority of the students in both classes . . . said that they could participate more in class discussions. What I realized from this is that the "problem" I had with discussion in my class is felt by the students as well.

I see this student's recognition that "there are no magic answers" as an important and valuable insight. To the extent that this kind of discovery might lead to further research into the dynamics of class discussion, developing additional strategies for facilitating discussion and discovering ways to make meaning of the often complicated dynamics of class discussion, I value the work that she has done here. Still, I am left (as a reader of her reflection) in the same position I suspect that she found herself occupying—both she and her students want discussion to happen differently and nothing that surfaced in this particular classroom inquiry project seems to have facilitated such change. Thus, among the challenges of this project (in its current form) are both the limited likelihood that it will result in new strategies for classroom practice in the short term, and the necessity of preparing students (particularly those who are eager for practical advice) for the alternative kinds of knowledge about classrooms that this assignment *is* likely to generate.

Second, although I think the project (again, in its current form) might be too rigidly structured, I have experienced—with a more loosely structured peer observation assignment in a previous year—a breakdown in the activity when two students (each observing the other's classroom) felt that each had violated the terms of the classroom visit as they had agreed to it. The observed, in this case, felt that the observer interfered with her classroom and interacted with students in unproductive ways. The observer felt that he had acted well within the bounds of what the two of them had negotiated in advance of the classroom visit. In following up with the two of them (individually) afterward, the observer admitted to having prepared a little autobiographical sketch of himself as a means of introducing himself (as they had agreed) that also included a response to the reading that was due in class that day. Having discussed the reading in advance with the teacher, this observer felt that his own differing interpretation of the text ought to be "on the table" as he put it. What actually happened with this particular classroom visit—whose version is "right" or "true"—is impossible to know. That both had genuinely tried to follow through on the assignment as they understood it seemed clear to me. That the assignment had not prepared either of them well enough for the important work of classroom observation also seemed clear to me. Ultimately, this experience convinced me that students could benefit from more guidance regarding this work—in formulating workable and productive questions as well as developing note-taking strategies for use in classroom observations.[2] The stakes of this assignment can be quite high as the required work impinges on relationships that are forming between peer teachers and between teachers and students.

A final and important shortcoming of this assignment seems to me to be more difficult to address. As my earlier critique of the heuristics included in Keig and Waggoner suggest, specific and questionable relationships that are prevalent in the academy (between observing/"master" teacher and observed/ "apprentice" teacher, for example, or teacher as "transmitter" of knowledge and students as receptacles for that knowledge) can get reinscribed via classroom observation. One such relationship that surfaced in my reflection on students' responses to this assignment is that of teacher/teaching-centered observations versus learning-centered observations. In my experience with students last year (all of whom, without exception, did outstanding work on this project), nearly all of them began (and most ended with) a focus on the teacher and teaching

---

2. In revising the assignment, I considered three different possibilities for note-taking—strategies that I termed "criteria-based," "event- (or issue-) centered," and "time-sampling." Criteria-based methods of classroom observation begin from assumptions (or, ideally, actual conversations) about what constitutes good teaching and where one might find evidence of that over the course of a class meeting. A frequently cited example of this approach is Sorcinelli's "classroom observation guide" reprinted in Keig and Waggoner. Under the heading of "Teacher's Knowledge of Subject Matter" are ten questions that focus attention on different observable aspects of the classroom such as "Does the material covered relate to the syllabus and goals of the course? Does the instructor present the origin of ideas and concepts? Does he or she contrast the implications of various theories?" (Keig and Waggoner 46). Issue- or event-centered observations derive from the goals of the observation. Thus, an observer focusing on how the teacher discusses student writing will attend to any moments in the classroom where student writing is explicitly or implicitly addressed. Both of these note-taking methods seemed to require that observers make quick judgments about the relationship between what they were seeing and the goals the group had for classroom observation. I thought it important to reserve that moment of judgment for later—to make that moment of judging the relevance of their observations part of the collective conversation and follow-up. Thus, I preferred time-sampling.

practice.[3] In retrospect, I think the structure of this assignment turned students toward an examination of teaching (more than learning) and this focus resulted in versions of classroom and education that were teacher-centered. To an extent, this focus might reflect the seminar participants' own interests and concerns as new or less experienced teachers. However, through the insightful objections raised by Rose Rodriguez-Rabin and Daniel Justice, both seminar participants and experienced advocates of tribal pedagogies, I came to see this phenomena as more than simply the result of the inquirers' interests. Some of the earliest and most enduring efforts to make teaching visible place the teacher at the center of the classroom. Efforts at documenting teaching not only risk reinscribing that teacher-centeredness but locate, in the teacher, the power and responsibility for what happens in the classroom. For these two seminar participants whose commitments to teaching were based in tribal understandings of power and educational relationships, a teacher cannot unilaterally decide to involve the class in a research activity that fundamentally changes the constitution of the group. Partly, the concern comes from respecting the quality and kind of work the class has already undertaken. I will leave the development of this particular argument to these two teachers who are working out, in the context of their own scholarship, a more nuanced and fluent account of their experience with this assignment and its implications for understanding *as culturally specific* the dominant structures of education that shape assessment practices. For my purposes, this extended example serves as additional evidence of the complex legacy of the movement to document teaching. As others in this volume have noted (for instance, Willard-Traub, Fox), efforts to document teaching construct the autonomy and responsibility of individual teachers in ways that warrant further scholarly attention.

These limitations notwithstanding, it seems important to restate what is, for me, one of the most important benefits of this activity—that it draws teachers into teaching as a site of vital scholarly work. It offers us the kind of conversations outlined above—where some participants engage critically and productively with the structure of the assignment while others find important insights into such topics as the place of silence in the classroom. It creates a shared sense of commitment to the intellectual work of teaching writing and the challenges of developing classroom practices that enact what we, as teachers, have learned about the teaching of writing. To some extent, this assignment addresses a further challenge. With increasing calls to document teaching and make sense of others' efforts to document their work as teachers, faculty (even

3. It is important to note the comments of Karen Head who, upon reading an earlier draft of this chapter, suggested that this interpretation of the students' work might be the result of my relying so heavily (and by necessity) on the textual artifacts produced as a result of this assignment. Echoing another student quoted earlier in this chapter, Karen suggested that had I been present during the students' discussion of the assignment and their observations, I would have had a different sense of their work.

those who are early in their careers) need opportunities to engage in this work and discover, for themselves, its power and limitations.[4] Writing about the need to offer teachers this kind of experience early in their development as teachers, Carolyn Frank (1999) explains that too many inexperienced teachers and readers of teaching documentation will, in her words "assume they understand the generic when it is the specific that gives classrooms their identity" (83). This activity, as many of the voices captured in this essay suggest, rendered visible this aspect of classroom teaching and, perhaps in that way, drew students into classroom observation as a means of gathering and reflecting on information about the teaching of writing.

Beyond Teacher Education: Observation and the Measure of Teaching

In a 1998 survey of liberal arts colleges, a full 40.3 percent of the responding institutions reported "always using" classroom observations in evaluating teaching performance—up more than 35 percent from a similar 1978 survey (Seldin et al. 14). Initiatives such as AAHE's Peer Review of Teaching Project (established in 1994) are thriving, enjoying widespread public and academic support and disseminating resources and model practices for documenting teaching (including peer observations of classrooms) nationwide. More modest in scale (but even more widespread) is the increasingly common practice of using classroom observations to gather data for letters of recommendation. Writing in the *ADE Bulletin,* Maura Ives (2000) argues that anyone who has agreed to write a letter of recommendation ought to address the quality of the candidate's teaching, observing at least one class meeting (in order to offer detailed support of the candidate's teaching strengths) and being "sure to mention" the classroom visit in the letter (46). If the data that Seldin and his associates collected and this anecdotal reference by Ives are accurate predictors, classroom observation plays an increasingly important role in formal assessments of teaching effectiveness in postsecondary institutions.

---

4. One limitation may be departmental structures that distract faculty from representing teaching as scholarly work. In reflecting on whether the "Collaborative Classroom Inquiry" project influenced her approach to writing the "course narratives" required of all teachers in the English department, seminar participant Rochelle Harris surmised that it did not (although she did incorporate aspects of the activity into her final seminar project and revised that project for publication): "I keep wondering why the peer observation activity—which is very similar in nature to the [required] reflections—didn't even get a nod in my writing about these two classes." Harris identifies several possibilities and concludes: "It could be that the blue sheet [departmentally mandated prompts for reflection on coursework and student evaluations] didn't trigger my thinking in a way that led me to incorporate the effect of the peer observation activity. My funding is temporary, so I saw the blue sheet as a document that was part of an argument to renew my funding. Another way to say that is the blue sheet was interpreted by me as an evaluative, institutional moment, not an opportunity to document teaching."

The approach to classroom observation outlined in this essay has been framed in terms of an assignment where course goals include introducing students to the teaching of writing as a site of scholarly work. However, the underlying principles of this assignment have proven useful to me as I take on increasing amounts of classroom observation for the purposes of writing letters of recommendation. In nearly every case, candidates (requesting a letter of recommendation) and I engage in a scaled-down version of the collaborative classroom inquiry detailed in this essay. We meet for a half hour to share syllabi and discuss our pedagogical interests; we each visit the other's classroom (usually only once); and, we write informally to one another about our observations and reflections on the class meetings. Not only does this structure allow me (as the letter writer) to garner the kind of detailed support that Ives recommends, but over the course of even this short interaction I gain useful insight into the candidate's pedagogical interests and habits of mind. (See the Website for examples of my observation notes and resulting discussion of a candidate's teaching in a letter of recommendation.)

If this essay has made some resources available to others in composition with an interest in classroom observation—particularly those whose work in composition includes teacher development—it also attempts to render visible significant limitations in generic approaches to classroom observation as applied to postsecondary writing classrooms. Structures for classroom observation that relegate "the observed" to a passive role or that set in motion a kind of master/apprentice model seem particularly troublesome for composition. As a field that has only recently enjoyed widespread institutional recognition (in the form of more faculty lines and such) and where a disproportionate amount of the teaching is carried out by graduate students, part-time faculty, and untenured faculty (the teachers most likely to find themselves cast in the role of apprentice), composition has a political stake in questioning such structures. Moreover, a considerable body of composition scholarship is dedicated to debunking the master/apprentice binary and its long hold on traditional thinking about teaching and learning. Another significant limitation of generic approaches to classroom observation surfaces in the often noted concern most recently recast by Deborah DeZure (1999), who warns that much of the research on teacher effectiveness "reflect[s] the long-standing hegemony of lecturing. . . . Care should be taken to use observation protocols that do not privilege lecture as the sole or best approach and that can be related to other modes of instruction" (88). Because theories of literacy learning, textual analysis, and intellectual growth through reading and writing are central to the organization of English courses in particular, we in composition (and in English studies more generally) need to develop ways of conducting classroom observation that are responsive both to the specific demands we face and the capacities we hope to sponsor.

7

The Course Portfolio: Individual and Collective Possibilities

Amy M. Goodburn

As the opening chapters in this collection have already outlined, many of the national calls to document postsecondary teaching have focused on the genre of the teaching portfolio (Edgerton, Hutchings, and Quinlan 1991; Seldin 1991). More recently, the genre of the "course portfolio" has emerged as a means of making visible the work of postsecondary teaching. While a *teaching portfolio* provides a broad vision of a particular teacher's goals, practices, and philosophies, the *course portfolio* represents a teacher's experiences with the significant moments, productive tensions, and assessment of student learning from the life of one course. William Cerbin (1996), one of the earliest advocates of the course portfolio, compares the teacher to a social scientist who views a particular class as a setting for investigating teaching questions. To conduct such an investigation, Lee Schulman (1998b) offers the guiding question "What can one ask about a course in order to understand the ways in which its creation and conduct constitute a coordinated act of scholarship?" (7). Randy Bass (1999) describes his approach to creating course portfolios as an "inverted pyramid" where the problems he poses about the teaching of his course lead him to reflect upon "the match between vision, practice, and outcomes" within a course (5). While the formative and summative tensions of self-presentation posed by teaching portfolios apply equally to course portfolios, advocates view course portfolios as a means to investigate and address problematic issues in one's teaching rather than simply prove one's successful teaching of a class. Bass writes: "How might we think of teaching practice, and the evidence of student learning, as problems to be investigated, analyzed, represented, and debated?" (2). Mariolina Salvatori (2000) suggests further that the best questions for a course portfolio are those that connect to our disciplinary conversations:

... teachers should ask questions about their students' work that grow out of their theoretical background; they should read and engage their students' texts by asking of them the same kinds of questions they ask of the scholarly texts they read and write. In addition, they should question the theories they espouse in terms of how they affect and reflect their students' learning. (84)

What constitutes a course portfolio is as diverse as the teacher teaching and the course being taught. In *From Idea to Prototype: The Peer Review of Teaching* Pat Hutchings (1995) describes three common elements of a course portfolio: 1) description of the course design, 2) description of the enactment or implementation of the design, and 3) analysis of student learning resulting from the first two dimensions. Materials collected for a course portfolio usually include some variation of the following:

> Sample course syllabi, assignments, and prompts
>
> Descriptions of methods used (peer response, discussions, conferencing, and so on)
>
> Results of students' evaluations with reflective commentary about them
>
> Samples of student work with reflective teacher annotations
>
> Responses to student work/statements of criteria for evaluation
>
> Author's notes focusing readers to particular features in the portfolio

In this essay, I discuss my experiences with developing course portfolios and how my uses of this genre have changed over the trajectory of my teaching life. In highlighting the varied and multiple purposes for my own uses of course portfolios, I hope to demonstrate that while individual institutional contexts may require particular "contents" for the documentation of teaching, teachers can be strategic in using such requirements for their own needs and purposes. Some of my purposes for course portfolios have included reflecting upon my growth and development as a teacher, identifying needs for curricular and programmatic revision, assessing and evaluating student learning, and intervening in department culture regarding pedagogical approaches. More recently, I was challenged to focus explicitly on assessment of student learning when I produced a course portfolio in collaboration with department colleagues. In drawing from these varied experiences, I hope to provide suggestions—and caveats—for postsecondary writing teachers interested in using course portfolios to represent their teaching.

The Course Narrative

My introduction to course portfolios began when I was given a Department "blue sheet" in my students' evaluations at the end of my first semester of teaching. The form consists of two sections: 1) "Commentary (evaluation of one's own performance and the class's performance)" and 2) "Assessment of the students' evaluations" (to be completed when the students' evaluations are returned the following semester). In addition, faculty must submit a syllabus, the students' evaluations, and a grade distribution for each course. While this form is idiosyncratic to my own department, its use spurred me to create what I would later come to call "course portfolios" for all the classes I teach. Thus, my entry into developing course portfolios was not based on national conversations about the scholarship of teaching but rather an institutional requirement to write a narrative about each course I teach.

Initially I found this requirement daunting. Although I had compiled a teaching portfolio during graduate school—replete with a teaching philosophy statement, sample syllabi, and student evaluations—I had never been asked to write reflectively about a particular course. One colleague shared her own course narratives as a model, but for the most part, I was on my own. Since that semester, I've written narratives for over thirty classes, and I've come to rely upon them as a critical record of my teaching development and as a vital component of the course portfolios I create. While what I write about depends upon the particular course, these narratives tend to run from three to six typed pages, and I usually organize them by categories such as "Strengths of the Class," "Issues that Arose," "Overall Goals/Purposes," and "Assessment of Student Work"(see the Website for course narratives from two classes).

The most basic way I use narratives within course portfolios is to articulate goals for my pedagogical choices, to describe student performance in response to these goals, and to revise assignments and course design based on this assessment. Much of this writing is, by necessity, couched in the discipline of composition. For instance, in the following excerpt, I assess student learning within a first-year writing course:

> One area that I need to continue working on is helping students develop interpretive writing skills, particularly when they are integrating others' voices as sources into their own arguments.... While these students were generally proficient at the mechanics of citing sources (creating a works cited page or using quotation marks within the text, for instance), they were not skilled in incorporating these sources in rhetorical ways.... So it's important for me to slow down their writing process at this stage and to provide more rhetorical strategies to help them engage with their sources rather than just cite them.

While this excerpt identifies an area on which I need to focus to support student learning, it also reflects disciplinary conversations about the teaching of writing, with all that the term "rhetorical" implies. So apart from describing students' performance on a particular assignment, this narrative also suggests particular disciplinary philosophies that I draw upon more generally to teach. After teaching a course several times, these narratives can be read for patterns that help me to reconsider course design more broadly. For instance, in writing about an advanced composition course that I was teaching for the third time, I outlined previous issues of concern and discussed how I addressed them:

In my previous two 354 commentaries, I noted several areas for improvement:
1) connecting response journals more fully to formal writing assignments;
2) incorporating a more diverse array of revision activities, 3) creating opportunities for more "creative" writing within the framework of the course focus
on argument, and 4) developing a fuller sense of community in an individualistic workshop setting . . . .

One area that I sought to improve upon was use of assigned reading in
connection to their writing. This semester I chose three books . . . to represent
a variety of ways that writers participate in public and academic argument. . . .
I chose this combination of texts because I wanted to illustrate how argument
crosses genre boundaries in both personal and public contexts.

Later in this narrative, in responding to the students' evaluations, I returned to
the issue of text selection by profiling students' responses:

> . . . many students cited the assigned readings as one of the aspects of the
> course that most helped them to learn. One wrote "The readings were terrific—
> they approached writing from many different angles." Another wrote: "I was
> most aided by the various types of persuasive readings we did—by seeing
> the examples." And a third said: "The books were good examples of what we
> were trying to accomplish in our papers." The previous two times that I have
> taught 354 with a focus on argument, students have complained about reading
> books in a composition class (and one student's evaluation this semester did say
> "Please do not make this class read so many books. This is a *writing* class.". . . .
> I was more deliberate about creating discussion questions and response journal
> prompts that explicitly connected the assigned reading to their own writing.
> Although their formal writing did not ask them to write *about* the books, I
> did emphasize how the books served as rhetorical models and as examples of
> various writing projects that students might take up.

In this excerpt, I present students' responses as both an affirmation of the
"success" of my book selection as well as an explanation of my pedagogy,
highlighting how I see the course texts and the assignments supporting each
other.

I also use course narratives to explore more serious problems that arise
in my teaching. After teaching a new course titled "Literacy and Community
Issues," I questioned how the internship component contradicted, rather than
extended, the students' learning:

> . . . many students experienced dissonance in how literacy was defined in their
> internships vs. what we, as a class, named and valued as literacy. In analyzing
> this tension, one student described the class as a "discussion or inquiry" about
> literacy where we focus on asking questions—"How is literacy connected to
> community? What are the ethics involved in literacy learning and in literacy
> work? . . . [yet] a student who designed a web page for the Lincoln Literacy

> Council struggled between using the organization's discourse to further the goals he believed in while . . . questioning the middle class values and "directive" literacy messages that he believed the organization was sending.

By focusing on students' final reflections about their internships, I was able to identify a central concern that pushed me to think harder about the underlying structure of the course. This narrative also cycled into my research, leading me to write a collaboratively authored essay with a graduate student who took the course in which we examined concerns with service learning inquiry in composition literature more generally (Ball and Goodburn 2000).

Although I primarily use course narratives to investigate teaching issues central to my own concerns, I am always cognizant of how my writing functions rhetorically for readers within my department. I write these narratives with an eye toward informing (and perhaps changing) readers' attitudes. For instance, I frequently hear faculty say that composition courses are only about "personal" writing and that students in these courses are not taught to write critically or analytically about texts. Thus, when I write narratives, I frequently give examples of student projects, both to showcase the quality of their work (which I appendix in my course portfolios) *and* to intervene in this lore. For example, here is how I described student work within an advanced composition class:

> Students were practiced in summarizing another writer's argument and in responding to it, but they did not have experience in analyzing an argument in terms of how it is organized or in terms of the underlying assumptions upon which it is based. . . .
>
> For the final sequence, students were asked to become cultural critics as they analyzed one site of popular culture. . . . One student analyzed professional wrestling and its ritualized use of stereotypes (through costumes, drama, etc.). Another analyzed the *Jerry Springer Show*, particularly in terms of its violence and its appeal to women and children at the battered women's shelter where she works. Another student who was planning her wedding analyzed the appeals and assumptions about weddings that are produced in magazines related to the wedding industry.

I can read the above passage as having multiple purposes. First, I am providing an assessment of students' performance, focusing on how I can encourage development of their analytical skills. I also describe students' topics to illustrate that students *can* write analytically and critically about *their own* experiences, to counter the criticism against approaches used within my and others' writing classes. In retrospect, I can read this desire to intervene in the department culture surrounding teaching in many of my course narratives. In fact, as I review the course narratives I've produced in the past seven years, I can see this "interventionist" purpose becoming more pronounced in my writing. Taken together, these course narratives provide a record of how my activist orientation to teaching has emerged and developed, and they show how my commitments to particular pedagogies have deepened.

Analyzing Student Performance

After six years of writing course narratives and collecting models of student work for my course portfolios, I was comfortable in how I documented my teaching. So when three colleagues and I were chosen to represent the English department in the UNL Peer Review of Teaching Project (PRP) for the 2000–2001 academic year, I didn't seriously consider how my documentation practices might change. But participating in this project challenged me to focus more concretely on how my students' work connected to my course goals and illuminated how conversation about course portfolios with colleagues can promote programmatic and curricular work.

The PRP is designed to "support faculty in the development of a community of scholars who write about the intellectual work involved in their teaching and who share that writing with interested colleagues" (UNL 1).[1] Each year, faculty work in department teams to develop individual course portfolios based on a series of memos called "interactions." Faculty post these three interactions on an electronic discussion board for review and response by other project participants and, at the end of the spring semester, they meet in a one-week workshop to discuss literature on the scholarship of teaching and to finalize their portfolios. The course portfolios are then made available for review by faculty on other participating campuses. The ultimate goal of this project is to "help faculty become skilled as writers and readers of course portfolios, making these portfolios useful both to those who produce them and those whose teaching can benefit from reading them" (UNL 1).

For the PRP, I wrote about a course that I was teaching for the second time: Reading Theory and Practice. This course is one of a set of courses required for preservice English/Language Arts majors in the Teachers College. A main goal of this course is to invite students to reflect upon their reading experiences and to help them imagine their teaching identities. Writing the first and second peer review project interactions[2] was easy because they followed the model that I had previously used in my course narratives. It wasn't until I wrote the third interaction—an analysis of student learning—that I was challenged to think about how adding this dimension to my course portfolio could radically change my teaching.

For the PRP's third interaction, participants were asked to analyze student learning based on one assignment. Questions to consider included goals/expectations for the assignment, the criteria used for evaluation of student

---

1. In 1994, University of Nebraska-Lincoln joined eleven other universities in a national Peer Review Project organized by the American Association for Higher Education (AAHE).
2. See the Website for the three UNL Peer Review Project interaction prompts.

performance, an analysis of the students' performances, and, finally, reflection about how this analysis informed my overall thinking with respect to the assignment and the larger course design. I chose to analyze three students' performances on a "Case Study of a Reader" project, the third and final project of the semester. As described in my portfolio:

> The case study of a reader project asks students to do a case study of a school-age reader over the course of several weeks. It builds upon the first two projects (a reading/writing history and an interpretive narrative) by asking students to 1) closely observe a reader within a school context, 2) collect the reader's writing about texts, 3) interview the student about his/her reading history, and 4) analyze the processes the reader uses in reading contexts.

I analyzed student performance on this assignment because I designed it to be a culminating moment that asked students to apply what they had been learning all semester. While the students' overall portfolios were a better marker of their individual learning in the course, I thought focusing on this assignment would help me assess what my students *as a class* were learning about reading theory and practice.

Articulating my criteria for this project was difficult because I assign holistic portfolio grades rather than individual grades for each assignment. Eventually, I brainstormed the following expectations for the case study project:

- Demonstrate a holistic understanding of the reader (in terms of processes, motivations, experiences, and abilities)
- Provide concrete evidence from the reader's experiences (class moments and interviews) to support this holistic analysis
- Integrate course material/terminology in analyzing the reader and in suggesting implications for addressing future students' needs
- Organize the data and analysis in a way that is reader-friendly (for example, using headings, an appendix, and so on)
- Reflect polished and edited prose

Simply creating this list forced me to articulate criteria that had not been available to my students when they were completing these projects. I saw how this list could have been incorporated within the actual project prompt (and could have alleviated some of the concerns students expressed as they were working).

More illuminating, though, was the process of writing a reflective analysis about *how* each of the three projects reflected "performance" based on a scale of low, middle, or high pass. In contrast to the summary of student projects I usually included in course narratives, this interaction spurred me to examine how the students' projects met the assignment criteria, forcing me to concretely articulate differences in the quality of their projects, and illuminating (somewhat painfully) the ways that students were not connecting the theories and practices we had studied in this assignment. Being asked to write concretely about my students' performances held me accountable in ways that writing my previous course narratives had not and opened up ways to reread my class design.

To illustrate, I provide excerpts from a final course letter I wrote to one student, Justin, about his project:

> It was fun reading about Mandy's experiences with and attitudes toward reading. She sounds intensely independent and honest. In terms of your analysis of her reading practices, there are several places where I, as a reader, wanted to see/hear more of Mandy's voice. You incorporate several strong quotes from her about her views toward reading and the class environment. Yet, as Jeremy suggested in his peer response to your initial draft, there are still several "Whys" to be answered in the text. For instance, there's not much about her actual reading process in terms of the strategies she uses to make sense of texts. And though you include concrete examples of Mandy's writing in your appendix, these materials aren't integrated within the text as a way of helping the reader see why they are important. There also are places in the conclusion that could be strengthened with references to some of the theories/ideas we've been discussing this semester.

This passage illuminates how I assessed Justin's project in terms of content and form, focusing on how his project performed in relation to an "ideal" case study. In contrast, my analysis of Justin's project offers insights into how the class, as a whole, responded to the project and the areas that I, as a teacher, need to rethink because of how students understood and enacted the project prompt. The following excerpt shows my analysis of Justin's project in comparison with the other two students' projects:

> Justin's project represents a middle pass (B/B− range). Justin is a strong writer who likes to explore ideas in a witty and casual style. He often digresses or goes on tangents as he unpacks ideas or makes connections to other ideas. . . . Justin's project does do a better job than Katie's of providing details that help represent Mandy as a reader. For instance, on pages three–four Justin describes Mandy's responses to an interview about her reading preferences, including titles of her favorite books and her motivations for reading more generally. Pages five–seven are probably the weakest section of Justin's project . . . because he doesn't incorporate Mandy's writing into his analysis. He does include samples of Mandy's writing in the appendix, but he doesn't make use of it in the project itself. Like Katie, Justin relies upon general statements without grounding his analysis with concrete evidence.

The degree to which I was able to articulate differences and similarities between the students' projects surprised me. I became more concrete, describing differences in their approaches and articulating the ways that I valued these differences in terms of my criteria for the project. Analyzing the students' projects in terms of my first two interactions showed me how I could refine assignments, by incorporating my criteria for evaluation in the original prompt, providing student models, and devoting more time to using observational class-room strategies. I also realized that I had missed a "teachable moment" for these preservice teachers in connecting this type of student assessment to their own future pedagogical practices.

Beyond revising how I teach the case study project, this analysis helped me to pose larger questions about my course design, such as "What does this project allow students to demonstrate about their learning? Does it enable them to syn-thesize their learning?" and "How might it *prevent* students from showing their learning?" These questions pushed me to consider the value of the assignment to begin with and to consider alternative ways for helping students to demonstrate "application" of course content. Writing about my students' performances also led me to consider how the sequence of courses for preservice English Edu-cation teachers could be more closely connected, such as through the use of collective projects that students could continue to work on throughout their English Education program. In sum, directly analyzing students' performances and writing about their learning in relation to course goals enabled me to gain insights about larger curricular and institutional issues that weren't visible when I wrote about my teaching more generally.

Using Course Portfolios for Programmatic Review

My participation in the PRP also taught me the value of conversations with col-leagues about course portfolios, even when the courses being profiled were not visibly connected in the curriculum. Although our department team's course portfolios represented a range of topics, approaches, and student experiences (Intro. to Critical Theory, Intro. to English Studies, and a senior/graduate semi-nar in British Romanticism), our team discussions usually centered on common goals and practices among our courses. Our course portfolios offered starting places for conceptualizing how to structure more integrated learning experi-ences for students. For instance, learning about how my colleague, Nicholas Spencer, introduces various philosophies toward reading in his critical theory course gave me insights into what students did and did not know about reading processes. We considered how this theory course, taken at the sophomore level, might better prepare students for my course. In a similar vein, my colleagues Chris Gallagher and Laura White discussed curricular connections between the Introduction to English Studies course and the British Romanticism sem-inar. These conversations were especially valuable because our department had just finished revising the undergraduate English major, creating two new courses (one of which was Intro. to English Studies) and developing concen-trations within disciplinary specialties. Our conversations about course port-folios provided a broader vision of the types of pedagogical practices and as-sumptions underpinning all our courses and much needed opportunities for conversation *across* our disciplinary specialties. Our conversations were so productive, in fact, that we were asked to share our insights at a department meeting.

Developing a course portfolio for review *outside* of my department also forced me to think about the tensions involved in articulating how my teaching is implicated in disciplinary knowledge and methodologies. My course portfolio became, in a sense, an argument not only for what *I* do in the classroom but also an argument for the *disciplinary* work valued in composition. While such conversations were sometimes frustrating, they provided me with opportunities to inform colleagues proactively about my students' writing rather than be in the role of defending my pedagogy against the common criticism "Why don't English teachers teach students how to write anymore?" Sharing course portfolios with faculty in political science, management, and anthropology offered me the teacher change-agent role that Cathy Fleischer (2000) advocates in *Teachers Organizing for Change*. I was able to showcase student writing and explain the rationale for my curriculum and pedagogy in ways that were understandable to broader audiences.

Suggestions and Caveats

Thus far I've outlined the benefits I've experienced in creating course portfolios, but there are limitations as well. As with any portfolio, teachers need the freedom and support to develop their own purposes for course portfolios, particularly if they are writing about problems or tensions arising in their teaching. While not all teachers in my department use course portfolios, I don't fear penalty for writing about problems that arise in my teaching. For instance, in my portfolio I discussed several tensions between my expectations and student responses that led, in part, to low end-of-the-semester evaluations. Reading about these difficulties led my department chair to write, "I will just comment that I sympathize with your problems with 476, having had a similar experience with a course required of Teachers College students some years ago" (May 24, 2001). He then elaborated on some of the issues he faced in teaching this course. My chair's comments reflect the type of supportive atmosphere teachers need in order to use course portfolios most profitably.

Perhaps the second most critical issue teachers face in creating course portfolios is time. It's difficult to write reflectively about one's teaching while also developing lesson plans, making handouts, and responding to student writing. At best, I can do one course portfolio a semester. I also find it difficult to represent the range of my students' learning without overloading the portfolio. In the course I profiled, students wrote four major projects, participated in a service learning project, wrote weekly informal writing, and participated in class writing activities. With each student's portfolio bulging at over a hundred pages, I could not possibly represent all their work. The practices most commonly used within composition (portfolios, multiple drafts, and such) can, ironically, make it more difficult to present holistic pictures of student performance within a course.

Another limitation is that course portfolios are, by definition, course based, so they do not provide an opportunity to showcase other teaching-related work that compositionists frequently do (Fox explores related issues in Chapter 13). This issue is especially important to composition teachers whose teaching often involves contexts outside of the classroom (workshops for teaching assistants, service-learning projects with community members, writing center administration, and so on). To address this issue, I added another section that outlines my broader teaching contributions via bulleted summaries of university and community-based projects.

Finally, course portfolios are only as powerful as the audiences for whom they are produced. Teachers can use course portfolios to reflect upon their own development as teachers—which is certainly important—but without an audience of other readers, course portfolios are a limited means of intervening in departmental or institutional cultures surrounding teaching. While I may write course narratives with the goal of intervening in commonplace attitudes about writing, for instance, simply writing such a narrative does not ensure that these attitudes will be dispelled. At their best course portfolios offer a way for teachers to articulate pedagogy, analyze student performance, and converse with fellow teachers about curriculum design and its enactment as a means of assessing and improving student learning. The most powerful uses of course portfolios come when they are read, assessed, and used in a community of colleagues. It is in these discussions that course portfolios have the potential to shape—and intervene in—departmental and institutional cultures of postsecondary teaching.

PART II

Implications for Documenting Teaching: Assessment, Evaluation, and Reform

8

Beyond Course Evaluations: Representing Student Voice and Experience

Margaret K. Willard-Traub

A year before finishing my degree and going on the job market, I had the pleasure of teaching a composition course with Robert.[1] In addition to being an exceedingly conscientious student, Robert had the habit of always extending his hand to me at the end of our formal conferences and informal conversations after class. Reflecting now on those handshakes, I remember having a sense of something very different in Robert's attitude toward our relationship, and more broadly in his attitude toward his own educational experience: yes, we were a teacher and a student, with vastly different responsibilities and positions within the institution. Yet Robert's proffering a handshake communicated to me that we were also partners in a sense: learning from and teaching each other, engaged together in what Paulo Freire would term "problem-posing" education, acknowledging our collaboration with a handshake. To this day, I have not had a student who so consistently and concretely embodied for me the notion that I am, in my most effective teaching moments, a learner and my students' collaborator.

When I went on the job markct, I was mindful of selecting documents that would represent some of the best consequences of my collaboration with students. Most of the jobs for which I applied (Research I and II institutions) did not specifically request that I document my teaching in the initial dossier, much less that I forward a lengthy teaching portfolio. When advertisements explicitly mentioned teaching, they typically made the less specific request for

---

1. Students' names have been changed in the interests of confidentiality and in concert with their requests at the time they consented to my use of their writing.

"evidence of effective teaching." As a result, I assembled a collection of materials to highlight my strongest commitments as a teacher. Although this collection did not comprise a "portfolio" in all the ways that other collections might, it accurately conveyed the values underlying my practice as a teacher. I included a teaching philosophy statement that supported the discussion of teaching in my letter of application; a dissertation abstract that reenvisioned the concerns raised in the teaching philosophy statement; and several student-authored texts that exemplified what I hoped to accomplish with students in my introductory writing courses. (See the Website for full texts.)

The commitments I most wanted to foreground through these documents were collaboration, reflection, and revision. I continue to believe that these are interdependent and crucial elements of education as "liberatory practice" (hooks 1994, 134), both for my students and me. In addition, I wanted my teaching documents to convey my belief in teaching as intellectual work, so they had to "speak to" the other pieces in my dossier that focused on scholarship. In giving meaning to and (as Bakhtin might say) "interanimating" each other, the documents describing my teaching and research would thereby challenge the long-standing dichotomy of teaching and research in higher education. For example, in my teaching philosophy I wrote that "in both beginning and advanced courses ... my teaching practice acknowledges the classroom as a scene of both intellectual work and complex relationships. I ask my students to see themselves not only as 'collaborators' with the authors of the texts we read, but as collaborators, too, with each other and with me." A concern for the varied kinds of relationships between writers and readers implied by this statement is also prominent in my dissertation, "Interanimating Voices: Theorizing the Turn Toward Reflective Writing in the Academy." My dissertation abstract, included in the job dossier, describes my project as focused on diverse examples of professional and student-authored "reflective" writing—"that is, writing that is explicitly reflexive with regard to the subject position of the writer, and that also functions to establish a relationship between the writer and her or his (oftentimes multiple) audience(s), in a way that underscores literacy as a social practice." I represented my research as well as my teaching, therefore, as theorizing how diverse "voices" (for example, of writers, readers, scholars, teachers, students) function in relationship with each other—collaborating with or animating each other—within the contexts of classrooms as well as texts. I argued that it was only through such collaboration or interanimation that subaltern perspectives— such as those of women, people of color, the poor, and others too often excluded from the cultures of power—might "sound" within traditional (institutional and discursive) contexts.

If including examples of student writing in representations of my teaching was imperative for me given the theoretical traditions I claimed for my scholarly work as researcher and teacher, it also raised challenging, ethical questions. Inscribing other voices into any "text" of my own, for whatever purpose, demands that I be accountable for conveying the autonomy or integrity of these other perspectives. In the case of students and a job dossier, however, these demands are particularly vexing because I am portraying these other perspectives as products of students' *collaboration with me*. Furthermore, the task of attending to the autonomy of student voices is complicated by the primary purpose underlying the collection of documents in which they are included: to "sell" the "good" of *my* experience and expertise as a teacher to hiring committees. The ethical challenge as I saw it then, given the audience and purpose for these documents, was for me to inscribe the work of students in a way that would suggest my expertise as a teacher, *as well as* students' expertise *independent of me*.

One way I addressed that challenge was by choosing examples of reflective writing that foregrounded the differences between students' subject positions and my own so that readers might be less likely to assume that students' expertise was *entirely* (or even primarily) a result of their working with me. While there were many shared intellectual interests and connections between my personal experience and those of the two students whose work I most frequently shared with hiring committees (in particular our working-class and urban backgrounds), there were also many differences (for example, race/ethnicity, age, experiences with schooling, and so on). At the same time, choosing to include in my dossier examples of reflective writing by students who foregrounded their experiences as African Americans required that I address the risk of co-opting (or appearing to co-opt) their perspectives simply to seem inclusive. Thus, the other documents I included in my dossier had to support the inclusion of these students' perspectives as uniquely illustrative of the ways in which my teaching and my scholarship—and the commitments underlying them—were interdependent.

Learning From Students: Representing Multiple Voices, Enacting Accountability

By definition, undergraduate students write at the margins of the academy. Yet students, too, are often required to compose portfolios or other collections of their work that represent diverse voices. Studying many different examples of student portfolios in the context of my doctoral work taught me much about the practice and ethics of incorporating diverse student voices within a representation of my own pedagogical practice, and indeed about the ethics of knowledge-making within the academy more broadly. In other words, by incorporating multiple voices within representations of my teaching I was following the lead of my students who themselves often composed multivoiced portfolios or other kinds of texts. The entering students whose work I studied, for example, were required to submit portfolios of high school writing as part of our university's entrance assessment. This portfolio required that students inscribe a complex voice that simultaneously addressed both a familiar high school audience and, like the documentation of my teaching that I was preparing, an unfamiliar audience of university readers.

These beginning college writers also had to learn early in their careers to negotiate the unfamiliar discourses of an institution that often expects them to reshape their own ways of speaking and writing, and to "extend themselves, by successive approximations, into the commonplaces" (Bartholomae 1985, 146) of traditional academic discourse. For example, Marquita, a beginning university writer whose work I included in my dossier, explains that she writes both for her family and for an institutional audience comprised of her peers and teacher:

> The purpose of my first piece on Harlem was to show how from generation to generation, my family has seen how one city could change dramatically over time. I wanted to give a perception of Harlem from three different perspectives, one of my Grandmother, my mother and myself. Through interviews and personal experiences I was able to grasp an idea of what Harlem used to be like. . . .

Like Marianna De Marco Torgovnick in her autobiographical essay, "On Being White, Female, and Born in Bensonhurst" (an essay our class had read as part of our work together), Marquita uses the changing identity of a place as a focal point around which to organize her inscription of multiple voices of family and community members.

Her determination that "the identity established by Harlem residents of the past" not give way to a completely new identity for her hometown, however more economically advantaged that new identity might be, is perhaps directly related to Marquita's determination that the voices and individual histories of her grandmother and mother not be silenced or erased:

> The Harlem Renaissance sparked an interest in my grandmother, an Alabama native to move north. In the south, Harlem was a place that black people dreamed about. A place where you could freely express your feelings as an African American and where African American culture was appreciated. . . . She loves Harlem and no matter how bad it gets, she refuses to leave. . . . "I see lots of promise here, I just can't see myself leaving when so much is about to happen. I feel a responsibility to see this community through and help in any way I can in its progress" (Brown, interview).
>   . . . .
>   My mother grew up in Harlem during the Civil Rights movement. Things that I read about in history books were part of her life. . . .
>   Harlem means so much to my mother. She loves the place where she grew up. I enjoy walking in Harlem with my mother, because she can point out and explain how beautiful Harlem used to be. I try to grasp that picture in my head.

In using interviews of family members and examples from personal experience along with other textual resources, Marquita succeeds in being accountable in her writing to "official" histories of Harlem that routinely represent the voices of public figures like Langston Hughes and Malcolm X; she also succeeds in being accountable to the voices of intimate others such as her mother and grandmother (an accountability echoed in her grandmother's sense of responsibility to support the community's "progress"), and to the material histories and emotional lives of these family members.

In writing reflectively about her hometown within the context of an introductory composition course at a midwestern university, Marquita furthermore is accountable to the everyday realities of her own life, as she struggles against the possibility that she will forget what Harlem has meant for her growing up:

> Harlem, the gritty, impoverished and world renowned upper Manhattan community that played host to a Renaissance of black art, literature and music during the 1920's and 30's is cautiously embracing economic rebirth (Kirby 5A). . . .
>
> I hope that this redevelopment of Harlem does not change everything about the atmosphere of Harlem. Even though there seem to be many negative aspects about Harlem and the need for change is essential, I still love the whole atmosphere of my community. . . . After school, teenagers hang out on 125th Street to meet up with friends and just "kick it." The streets may not seem safe to an outsider and I can understand because there is a drug dealer on every corner and drug addicts are continuously begging you for change, but I feel a sense of security and protection because I am so familiar with the atmosphere. A mall in Harlem just does not seem right to me. . . . A change is necessary but I hope the right kind of change is made. One that does not erase the rich history of Harlem and what it means to African Americans.

Marquita's text is a testimony to the importance of Harlem's cultural survival for her own life as a "young black teenager"; it is accountable to her own voice, in other words, as is the reflective piece she wrote a year earlier to introduce her entrance portfolio, a piece in which she stated the hope that her readers would "get to know (her) on paper through (her) words" because of the ways in which she "wrote about experiences and ambitions that . . . shaped (her) into the individual (she was)."

Marquita's text is also a testimony to the importance of Harlem's cultural survival for the collective life of an African American community for whom it may still represent, as it did for her grandmother, "a place (to) dream about." Marquita's use of diverse audiences and voices may not represent the commonplaces of academic discourse; however, she does succeed in surrounding her discussion of Harlem's social and economic flux with several different narratives of material and emotional experience representing a heteroglossia of perspectives and her love for "the whole atmosphere" of her community. I wanted my dossier to follow Marquita's lead in this regard: any accurate representation of my teaching practice had to include several different narratives, and a mix of different perspectives.

But what did it mean that I, a white, (now) middle-class woman, inscribed Marquita's voice, the voice of a young, African American student, in the teaching materials I used while on the job market? What ethics were at work in such a representation, and what were some of the possible consequences of such an ethics? What I would like to suggest here is that while I in some way inscribed a (personal) relationship with Marquita by inscribing her voice (and the voices of those whom she inscribes) in the "text" of my dossier, I ran the risk of exploiting her voice and our relationship if I represented her voice *simply as evidence of my own accomplishment.* The question I had to answer—even if imperfectly—was whether or not it was possible to utilize Marquita's perspective without betraying the personal, and professional, trust inherent in her giving me permission to do so.

To suggest that such a complex and difficult task was indeed possible is also to suggest its critical importance in portraying the ethical and intellectual dimensions of teaching. In other words, I believed then, as I do now, that I had no choice with regard to including the voices of (diverse) others in any representation of my accomplishments as a teacher and a scholar. However, it also was true that I had no choice with regard to being reflective about *how and why I was including those voices.* And, in the absence of a full-blown teaching portfolio, this explanatory function fell to the teaching philosophy statement, the dissertation abstract, and the job letter.

These other documents served two purposes. First, they articulated my rationale for including (nonedited) student texts in my dossier. In the Statement of Teaching Philosophy, for example, I reference Richard Rodriguez's *Hunger of Memory* as comprising part of a "range of models for writing" that I offer to students. In this reference, I point to how Rodriguez's memoir itself represents multiple voices: certainly his own ("Rodriguez uses his own personal experience as a resource in order to come to some general conclusions about the effects of schooling and the aims of education"); as well as those of others ("Using Rodriguez's memoir again as a model, students can, for example, see how Rodriguez himself draws on other texts and perspectives in the course of constructing an analysis or argument"). Second, these documents served a (perhaps) more prosaic function: they represented a somewhat traditional approach to documenting teaching wherein authority (seemingly) is vested primarily in the job candidate. Since they could be read even in the absence of the student texts, these documents could meet at least some of the expectations of hiring committees unused to reading entire student texts as part of a job file.

Describing and Inscribing Voice: Documenting the Interanimation of Research and Teaching

In many ways, including students' voices in my dossier was necessitated by my expressed commitment to scholarly projects that attend to diverse perspectives and to cultivating a " 'responsive understanding' of the social world." The dissertation itself was, in large part, an exploration of the meaning of "voice" in student and scholarly writing. *In a Different Voice,* Carol Gilligan's (1982) seminal critique of the assumptions upon which psychological theories of the moral development of women have been constructed, begins with a definition of "voice" that challenges the modernist conception of a unified and stable "self." Gilligan's critique offers some insights into how and why a text—for example, a teaching portfolio or another collection of teaching materials—and the "self" it is said to represent, should be conceived of as multiple and dia-logical. Gilligan's concern for "the problem of interpretation" (2) in light of reconceptualizing "voice" as multivalent echoes Bakhtin's interest in the self as dialogic. "It cannot be stressed enough," writes Michael Holquist (1990) of Bakhtin "that for him 'self' is dialogic, a *relation*" (18–19). "[T]he self is like a sign," Holquist later explains, "in so far as it has no absolute meaning in itself: it, too (or rather, it most of all), is relative, dependent for its existence on the other" (35).

Representing the voices of others, especially those of students, is unavoid-able in efforts to tell adequately the "story" of one's teaching. For it is only in relation to the words (and experiences) of others that our own words have meaning. Like the complex compositions that comprise much current ethno-graphic and reflective scholarship across the disciplines, teaching materials can (and should) inscribe multiple voices, not simply the voice of the teacher. But with such an inscription come multiple relationships—between voices or per-spectives represented; the interests those perspectives might be said to serve; and the varied audiences addressed by such voices. These different sets of re-lationships thus unavoidably increase the intellectual and ethical complexity of our documentation practices.

Robert, the student whose handshake opens this essay, enacts via his writing a way of addressing such complexity. In an essay entitled "My Past," as part of the work required for composing his own course portfolio, he writes:

> Unlike (Richard) Rodriguez, I have not achieved the "end of educa-tion".... I am still changing, still in search of a true identity as an American citizen. As a student of the University of Michigan I still search my psyche for confirmation of my identity. Do I embrace my blackness, hold on to my rich African heritage; or do I assimilate into the European value system? Is it possi-ble for the descendant of slaves to become an All-American boy? Can such an individual as an All-American black boy exist in 21st century America? Per-haps time, together with education will cause the answer to emerge. Perhaps, I am still known as the neighborhood's "white boy."
>
> Choosing to come to U of M rather than Howard University or More-house, may have served to reinforce that stigma. Here, I may even be referred to as the "black boy" down the hall. The fact is, no other person nor group will define me. What I now know is that the pigmentation of one's skin, or lack of, does not define character, intellect nor dignity. These human qualities

must be established by each individual as his or her spiritual being dictates.
Each person must make the choice.

I would suggest that Robert has learned what Linda Brodkey (1996) says students most often are not taught—he has learned to write "on the bias," transforming the "threads" of his words into the "cloth" of language (50).

Robert's representation of his experience as complex, as comprising conflicts as well as accomplishments, is a representation that teaches me the value of telling stories of loss as well as of gain. Prompted to write reflectively, Robert recognizes the dichotomous world in which he lives without resorting to simple dichotomies, such as the belief that race is always the only (or even primary) dynamic shaping his relationships with his peers, a belief that he could (perhaps easily) oppose with the conclusion that race ultimately does not (or "should not") matter at all in how those relationships take shape. Instead, he recognizes that he is still, and simultaneously, the "white boy" in the neighborhood and the "black boy" at school; at the same time he is also the individual who "must make (a) choice," an individual whose "human qualities must be established . . . as his . . . spiritual being dictates." His posing the question of whether or not it is "possible for the descendant of slaves to become an All-American boy" acknowledges the legacy of war and racial violence and simultaneously looks to the future with a sense of other possibilities.

Within his course portfolio, Robert inscribes his subjectivity as both socially constructed and as freely chosen. Robert teaches me that the practice of composing a representation of my self and my voice involves representing the voices of others in ways that are responsive to history and to the diversity of experience within the current moment. Representing the diversity of experience within my classroom entails including the voices of students such as Marquita and Robert, students whose subject positions differ from my own in varied ways.

Including diverse student voices within my dossier was absolutely essential if my job materials were to support one of my stated goals for teaching and research: to enlighten the "practices of scholarship and of the teaching and assessing of academic writing, in ways that make these practices both more intellectually rigorous and more accountable to the concerns and needs of diverse student populations"—as those concerns and needs are articulated by students *themselves*. Both Robert and Marquita exhibit what I consider to be considerable strengths in their writing, articulating a self-consciousness about identity and about the complex legacies of their current perspectives. In addition, for beginning writers especially, both produce quite rhetorically sophisticated texts, moving between very different kinds of "data" that presumably will appeal to very different kinds of readers.

Because neither of these essays is error-free, however, including them in my job materials further enacts an "ethics of accountability," to a particular pedagogy and to my students. These student texts say something very important about my priorities as a teacher, and so I included them despite their potential for making me (and my expertise) more vulnerable to the critique of certain audiences. If as teachers we claim to value certain attributes in student writing, much less a student-centered and collaborative classroom, then I believe we are ethically obligated to make these commitments *concrete* by preserving the integrity of students' words and work within our teaching documentation. To do anything less is to risk reducing our representation to an unintellectual "packaging" of experience—essentially a cynical exercise in "rhetoric" that would deny the scholarship of teaching.

In examining how he is "still changing, (and) still in search of a true identity as an American citizen," Robert's text finally inscribes a kind of agency, as it works through (although not entirely explicitly or completely) a theoretical and "multi-sited" understanding of culture (including the variations in academic culture that exist among diverse institutions, such as Howard, Morehouse, and Michigan). Such an understanding, in turn, makes possible a mobilization in the text of what Patti Lather (1991) has termed "multi-sited agency" (121). And it is just such a multi-sited agency that is enacted by teaching documentation that includes diverse representations of students' voices, along with layered representation of a teacher's voice. In making choices about how to incorporate these varied perspectives, we might consider such a collection as "intransigently pluralist" to use Holquist's terms (35), and we might include such course artifacts as drafts of student writing, peer responses and reviews, notes from conference interactions, and email exchanges with individual students or excerpts from electronic discussions. These kinds of artifacts provide a range of voices in dialogue in ways that, for example, institutionally sponsored student evaluations alone do not.

Documenting Teaching and the Shifting Subject

This essay claims that representing a range of other perspectives within the context of teaching documentation ensures a more accurate portrayal of a teaching self. We cannot, as Bakhtin suggests, fully perceive ourselves: "For all of their comparative openness, indeed *because* of it, self-categories cannot do what categories of the other can. Seeing requires a certain outsideness to what is seen, a certain stasis" (Holquist 26). He argues, further, that "in order to see our selves, we must appropriate the vision of others" in large part because "existence, like language, is a shared event" (Holquist 28). Both Robert and Marquita have provided me with the reflective gaze of an other in my representation of teaching. Reflected in these others' gazes, and in the very different relationships I have shared with them, I have come close to seeing my own (contingent) self: a student who often has looked to the stuff of traditional schooling for answers to questions of identity; a scholar looking to the stuff of personal experience for making meaning out of history and culture; a teacher looking to both kinds of resources for guidance in creating opportunities for student learning.

The contingency of self that I see represented in both Robert's and Marquita's texts is central to both my scholarship and to my understanding of how to teach writing well. As such, it appropriately became one of the criteria I used to select the student texts I included in my dossier. Incorporating these texts into my job materials thus served two purposes: it was a means for being accountable to my beliefs and pedagogical practices; furthermore, it was a means for connecting my pedagogical practices to my scholarship. While other teachers might not find it appropriate or useful to use the same criterion in selecting student texts, I would argue it is essential to consider carefully how both the selection and the inclusion of student voices in a set of job materials help to represent the complexity of the intellectual work of teaching, as well as the richness of any candidate's preparation and abilities.

The increasing use of teaching and student portfolios in the academy as well as a trend toward valorizing representations of diverse selves and voices signify a shift toward a model of scholarship and teaching that emphasizes the ways in which *relationships* between the diverse voices of writers and readers, teachers and students, collectives and individuals, are established; and a model of literacy tied more closely to postmodern epistemologies that affirm the multiplicity and contingency of the self, and the "personal" realities of diverse individuals in relationships. In this way, representations of teaching that incorporate students' voices and experiences share common ground with Linda Brodkey's notion of autoethnographic texts that "do not attempt to replace one version of history with another, but try instead to make an official history accountable to differences among people that communitarian narratives typically ignore" (28).

Through documenting teaching I aim to be accountable, therefore, to my own (various) voices, to the diverse voices of others within the institution, and to the different ways in which all these voices interpret the world. Like Robert, however, being thus accountable for me has meant at times working against the grain of traditional notions of teaching and scholarship that dichotomize the two kinds of work, and that privilege a teacher's (unitary) voice above all others. But again, as Robert's text makes clear, the point of using an "I" that has both a specific history and an open future lies in interpretation. During particular moments in the process of assembling a dossier, as well as during particular moments interacting with students in the writing classroom or collaborating with other teachers, the rewards of such interpretive work for me have shone through. These are moments when, as bell hooks would term it, my own education has become "liberatory practice" (134). In such moments, I can actually feel my identity shifting—watching, for example, as students come to see through their writing something they had never seen before; watching myself, too, as I might have been, if my own history had been different; as I am today, seeing something brand new, reflected in the materials that represent my teaching self.

9

The Medium and the Message: Developing Responsible Methods for Assessing Teaching Portfolios

Chris M. Anson and Deanna P. Dannels

From its beginnings in the mid-1980s as a tool for promoting the "scholarship of teaching" (Boyer 1990) and providing a richer way to assess performance, the teaching portfolio spread to college and university campuses across the nation (see Anderson 1993 for representative accounts). Oddly, the initiative did not have its origins in the disciplines most closely associated with writing, even though teaching portfolios contain mainly written documents (Anson 1994). Instead, many English and composition faculty have been encouraged to develop teaching portfolios by nonwriting-specialists: university administrators, officers of evaluation, leaders of teaching and learning centers, or others involved in promoting and assessing the quality of undergraduate education. In such cases, a new, complex academic genre is introduced, in the hope of quick implementation and ready success, to whole departments of genre specialists, compositionists, rhetoricians, creative writers, linguists, and literary theorists.

In this context, the successful implementation of teaching portfolios soon can be hampered by apprehension and misunderstanding. In our consultations across the curriculum, we find that faculty in the humanities, particularly those who work extensively with written text, often are both the most insightful and the most uncertain adopters of teaching portfolios. Teachers and scholars of literacy are advantaged in their typically strong writing skills, interests in textuality, and complicated interpretive strategies. Yet these strengths also create unique challenges in the production and assessment of portfolios. The same skills that allow teachers in our profession to write elegant, sophisticated entries can also lead to idiosyncratic or deconstructive readings of portfolios—readings in which reaction to prose style (to take just one feature) can all but erase the focus on teaching. The result can be an unfair or uneven application of standards, subverting the goals of a portfolio program.

In this essay, we first explore several complexities in the evaluative use of teaching portfolios. For example, portfolio theory encourages teachers to take risks, experiment, and reveal uncertainty or failure in their portfolios. Yet it may be perilous to offer such disclosure in a portfolio that will be examined for positive evidence of success. A related problem concerns the way that teachers represent their instruction—in text or in other media—and what this representation implies for a process of fair evaluation.

We conclude with a turn toward the practical and strategic: what can departments, committees, and review teams in our profession do to ensure that we are applying the most consistent, insightful, and ethical standards to reading and judging teachers' portfolios? What can be done, even in the midst of an institutional interest in assessment, to create a culture of teaching and nourish both greater collaboration among faculty and more insightful, self-improving reflection in individual teachers?

The Problem of Evaluating Formative Entries

Teaching portfolios first appeared because of a justified belief that faculty and departments were not doing a good job of assessing the quality of their instruction. Student surveys, perhaps the most ubiquitous tool for evaluation on college campuses, inadequately reflect whether what happens in most classrooms is successful in promoting students' learning. Nor do they provide any information about a teacher's goals, attempts at self-assessment, or pedagogical insightfulness. Teaching portfolios offer instead "multiple measures" of a teacher's work, from a syllabus to a series of writing assignments to a reflection on an experiment in leading class discussion. The encouragement of rich description and sensitivity to context leads to "ecological evaluation" (Lucas 1988) or "authentic assessment" (Wiggins 1984); the emphasis shifts toward the enhancement of learning, "with the assessment of outcomes for purposes of accountability occurring only as a by-product" (Lucas 1992, 9).

Portfolios also allow teachers' performances to be evaluated in both "primary" and "secondary" documents (Anson 1994). Primary documents include the direct artifacts of a teacher's work—items that are required to do the job (such as a course syllabus). Secondary documents are commentaries and reflections on those primary documents, and on teaching more generally. Not normally required in the daily course of teaching, secondary documents take additional time to craft. But they also give faculty a way to explain the thinking that underlies their instructional decisions, and to explore, in reflective entries, the complexities of the teaching situation.

As portfolio systems were adopted to help teachers display the full spectrum of their teaching activities, it soon became clear to faculty developers that the process of preparing a portfolio (especially secondary documents) was, by itself, improving teaching. What began as a way to *evaluate* teaching soon took on new meaning and potential as a way to *develop and improve* teaching (Seldin and Annis 1992).

But the relationship between the formative and summative roles of portfolios has not been explored very fully in the literature on teaching assessment. Advocates of portfolios consistently argue the benefits of reflection, or "reflective practice" (Schön 1986, 1991) or "critical reflection"—"recognizing and generating [one's] own contextually sensitive theories of practice" through "continuous investigation and monitoring" of one's teaching (Brookfield 1995, 215). In the most supportive settings, faculty may feel at ease presenting portfolios that share doubts or reveal problems in teaching for the sake of reflection and improvement. Yet portfolios, as Shulman (1998) argues, also have a necessarily *public* function. As the evaluative stakes of this public function rise, and with them the chance that a faculty member's "flaws" are used against her, the portfolio can soon turn into a starker display of teaching; there is a stronger focus on the more "public" primary documents and less display of a teacher probing into her instruction in a reflective, scholarly way. If evaluators are looking for such evidence of reflection, however, the faculty member is caught in a double-bind, neither wanting to risk disclosure nor able to dispense with it.

An anecdote may be instructive. At one large midwestern university, an English department required its dozen temporary adjunct faculty to prepare portfolios for annual reviews, reappointment, and merit pay increases. One adjunct instructor had spent considerable time studying the literature on teaching portfolios and had even run some workshops on their principles and design. When it came time to submit her portfolio, she included several documents that explored concerns she had identified in her own teaching, and cited a handful of student evaluations that bore upon these concerns in specific but less than positive ways. In keeping with the formative principles of portfolios, she believed that exposing and reflecting on a problem in a recent course could show her as a teacher who thinks critically about her instruction and explores her individual approaches and classroom strategies (Duffy and Jones 1995, 21). Yet the department administrator, unschooled in the principles of portfolios and untrained to evaluate them, read these reflective entries as signs of weakness, and gave her the lowest possible rating. The teacher was presenting herself in "the best light"—as someone who "frame[s] and systematically investigate[s] questions related to student learning" (Hutchings 1998, 13). For the administrator, the teacher's "best light" would have been the surface display of unequivocal success.

Clearly, whether portfolios are to be more than a physical container of cursorily produced primary documents will depend critically on the values of those who encourage or require portfolios to be developed and those who reach judgment on their strengths and weaknesses. When the two contexts are the same (as in a department using teaching portfolios to promote teaching *and* to assess it), administrators must align these functions carefully and responsibly. When the two contexts are different (as in a teacher on one campus applying for a job on another), the portfolio creator needs to select and prepare entries cautiously, with full knowledge of the audience(s) the portfolio will address.

The Problem of Textual Representation

Like any written text, teaching portfolios involve rhetorical and linguistic decisions that reveal knowledge, imply or invoke particular audiences, and construct a persona. Further complexity arises when we realize that a portfolio is not so much a genre of academic writing but a collection of genres: narratives, teaching philosophies, speculative journal entries, course syllabi, assignment sheets, evaluative rubrics. Whatever we may glean from reading an entire portfolio comes from a tapestry of documents written under different circumstances and often for different audiences. While portfolios can give us a fuller picture of a teacher's work, they can just as easily manipulate our attention or create fictions. In the situation described above, it became clear to several of the adjuncts that the highest evaluations were not given to the "best teachers," but to those who had displayed their teaching in the slickest, least insightful, or probing ways.

  A related problem in the relationship between surface display and depth of ability or insight can arise when there are disjunctions between a teacher's knowledge and action, or between "knowing that" and "knowing how" (Ryle 1949). For example, a teacher can be more adept at explaining an approach than using it in her pedagogy. A literature teacher who has read about reader-based approaches to instruction, which lead to active classrooms involving students in the discussion and negotiation of disparate responses to readings, may be able to articulate those approaches more elegantly and convincingly than she is able to use them effectively in her teaching. The result is what we might call "passive endorsement"—a textual display of instructional knowledge in secondary documents that is instantiated weakly in practice. Consider the following excerpt from the portfolio of a faculty member in an English department, who is writing about an introductory literature course:

Sample Excerpt 1

The cultural politics of education provides a proving ground for democratic ideals of education, for liberatory education. I work from the vantage point of the classroom as *site* for the operation, and application, of such principles as those espoused most elegantly by Paulo Freire. Breaking down the boundaries of class and culture, of division and status, my classrooms become the source of a grand decomposition of assumptions about, for example, history as conquest (we think instead of oppression) and literature as a reflection of universal truths (we think instead of white, male, European). Nothing is taken at face value. Liberatory pedagogy allows for the contestation of values and schemes embedded deeply in what we read. By the end of my course, students are swimming in a world of new insight, and they begin to see that they are products of a system in which, in an Althusserian sense, if they are not part of the solution then they are part of the problem.

Readers of this teaching philosophy may be seduced by its elegant, if not entirely coherent, prose style, and by the sense that this is a teacher who is very much in command of his educational ideals. The reference to Freire and liberatory education might well set the savvy reader's head nodding in gentle agreement just as it might serve to confirm the less broadly read educator's belief that, yes, this faculty member seems to know what he's doing.

Also of interest in this excerpt is the relationship between theory and practice. In this case, the former heavily outweighs the latter: we learn almost nothing about what really goes on in this teacher's classroom. Pulled instead toward the ideals of New Historicism and revisionist approaches to literature, we construct our own image of classes abuzz with activity and energy. Yet there is little sense here of a teacher who is actively questioning or experimenting with his own teaching methods, or trying to assess the strength of those methods. Simply asking how a working-class student responds to the ideals of the course as the teacher describes it (see Seitz 1998) is enough to prompt considerable reflection or even more formal investigations of these ideals in the classroom.

The potential seduction of this entry illustrates a central problem when portfolios are understood to be textual records of belief, rather than mediators between belief and action. The statement, "I work from the vantage point of the classroom as *site* for the operation, and application, of such principles as those espoused most elegantly by Paulo Freire," compels readers to create a web of inference, a vision of a classroom in which students' own values and perspectives get artfully teased out in the context of discussion and negotiation—a classroom where students and their subjectivities matter. Sometimes the most glib and confident entries come from teachers so immersed in their own intelligence that, in practice, students have little or no voice at all. In the Freirean-inspired classroom may stand a teacher who daily enacts the "banking approach" to education: filling empty minds with little deposits of knowledge. Mutely, the students record information as fact. Far from swimming in worlds of new insight, they try to keep their heads above the murky waters of pedantry.

The risk of passive endorsement to fair evaluation increases in relation to the portfolio's distance from the context of instruction. Selected portfolio entries sent to a hiring committee at another institution can offer reviewers all the "right stuff" in the candidate's choice of terms or descriptions of principles, but there may be few opportunities to see those principles in action. As this risk increases with distance, so does the need for the portfolio to move back and forth between primary and secondary documents. Gaps in the connection to practice can be reduced when other entries, such as course syllabi or lesson plans, show how the philosophy is enacted. But clearly, the portfolio system must encourage teachers to create those links explicitly for the reader or evaluator, either between discrete documents or within them.

Sample Excerpt 2, for example, comes from a new Ph.D. seeking a tenure-track position (the entry describes one of the courses she designed and taught while serving as a teaching assistant). This writer had also participated in sessions examining the theory and practice of teaching portfolios.

Sample Excerpt 2

I designed *Knowledge, Persuasion, and Power* [title of course] with the aim of tightly integrating group-based projects and presentations with lectures and class discussions. This approach reflected my basic conceptual design for the course, which was to integrate interdisciplinary theoretical approaches to knowledge with the social practices of knowledge-production. Working in permanent groups with three or four of their peers, students were assigned collaborative projects that challenged them to think about and then articulate the ways in which forms of knowledge and knowing entered into their lived, social experience. Each group project culminated in a presentation to the rest of the class, and was followed by an opportunity for the group to discuss their work with the other students.

Here we see the application of an approach. In a few lines, we learn that the teacher makes use of small groups in socially dynamic ways; uses collaborative writing activities; weaves opportunities for public presentation into the fabric of her course; and includes time for both lecture and discussion. We learn further that these methods are informed by a philosophy, itself closely tied to the intellectual goals of the course: to help students to experience the "social practices of knowledge production" just as they investigate "the roles and functions that knowledge plays in modern society." As we read the rest of this and other entries, we see a teacher constantly working at the intersections of theory and practice, philosophy and action.

Less evident in this entry, however, is someone actively interrogating these intersections in a scholarly way. Even as teachers are encouraged to link reflection with action, knowledge with practice, theory with implementation, such links may still be insufficient to show whether particular methods are working. A true scholarship of teaching encourages teachers to become active investigators of their own instruction—classroom-based researchers posing and investigating important questions about the effectiveness of what they are doing. This need for experimentation and evidence has been shown to lead faculty into deeper and more productive thinking about their teaching (see, for example, *Carnegie Chronicle* 1999).

A Further Problem: Performance as Text

How many times have we tried to capture—after the fact—the transformative and magical nature of a classroom only to feel that there is no adequate way to re-present that temporal event? As Ong reminds us (1996), orality is transitory, contextual, and temporal. Every instructional message includes both content and relational dimensions (Watzlavik et al. 1967), a distinction that bears considerable exploration in a profession dominated by an ideology of "coverage" and a lack of interest in "method." The process of facilitating group work, mentoring students through writing assignments, and coordinating public presentations is embodied in a person—the teacher—whose communicative style is laden with relational cues only apparent in performance. The rich, face-to-face interaction that characterizes the classroom (Sproule and Kiesler 1986) allows for rapid feedback, utilizes both verbal and nonverbal channels, is typically accomplished in physical presence, and affords flexibility in the use of language. These performative aspects of teaching are, by nature, difficult to capture in the written texts we use to represent our teaching, no matter how accurately we may believe we are doing so.

Sample Excerpt 2, with its concrete description of teaching strategies, philosophies, and assignments, provides a clear picture of the structure of this teacher's classroom. Yet that picture still fails to capture the nature of teaching as a communicative process (Cazden 1988), as a process of performance and embodiment (Sprague 1993). Worse, it may represent those processes inaccurately. The nature of assessment, which privileges written text for reasons of convenience, a greater degree of objectivity, and a belief in legal permanence, confines that act to textual boundaries that do not do justice to these oral, embodied, and performative aspects of teaching.

We know, for example, that the teacher uses small groups, yet we learn nothing about how she crafts small-group activities in the lived, temporal moment. If a small group gets off track and begins discussing the latest news event or sporting victory, how does this teacher respond? Does she make the bold claim: "Group 1—get back on task..." or does she discretely drift over to the group and ask a question to focus their attention? When dealing with an elementary question, how does the professor respond? If she says, "You seem to be having a difficult time understanding the material," is her tone sarcastic, chiding, or concerned? How might she explain that tone if asked about it by a colleague who visited her class? While such questions may seem to focus on simple logistics or "classroom management," they are part of a deeper, organic system of socially negotiated identities and subjectivities.

Performance as text for teaching portfolio assessment presents us with both an opportunity and a challenge. Considering performance as text allows faculty and administrators to account fully for the contingent and contextual nature of classrooms. It also provides an avenue for faculty who are especially concerned about giving evidence for the synergistic, socially constructed space they call their classroom. Yet how do we capture performance as text for assessment?

The various answers to this question generate further complexities, such as the nature of authorship and representation. As teachers, we have probably all experienced confessing to a colleague that we had just taught the worst class in our lives, only to be met moments later by a student who found it really engaging. Power issues aside, this scene illustrates one of the problems of considering performance as text for teaching assessment—authorship. Who should represent it? Should our students be responsible for crafting evidence of the performative aspects of teaching? Should those aspects be explored through self-assessment and reflection? Or should others, perhaps peers, be entrusted to do the job?

In the English department of a midsized research-oriented university, for example, faculty are asked to include a colleague's written report of a classroom visit. Visits must occur once per semester. The person being observed can optionally comment and reflect on the observer's report. These reports and responses presumably encourage peer observation and show something more about teachers' classrooms.

In consulting with an administrator in this department, one of us examined sample observation reports and responses submitted by faculty for the process of annual review. The following is one such report, which was unaccompanied by a reflective statement.

Sample Excerpt 3

April 18. Visited [Smith's] Milton class. 28 students in attendance. Smith began with a discussion of an upcoming paper assignment. Students appeared to be attentive; a few asked good questions. This took 10 mins. Smith then lectured on *Il Penseroso* for about 35 minutes, doing a capable job of discussing issues of genre and the poem's place in the Milton canon. Last 10 mins. were given over to discussion. Several habitual responders, but the others looked interested and studious. In all, a quite informative class.

Without a clearly articulated system of observation—both developmental and evaluative—the efforts represented in this entry can become nothing more than an exercise in accountability. Neither the visitor nor the teacher has seized this opportunity to probe into the dozens of important issues of potential relevance to teaching and reflective practice—what to do to engage more of the students in discussion; how a good writing assignment is crafted, explained, and supported in classroom activities; or how lecture time might be reduced for more active learning strategies. Again, the values embedded in the larger system of assessment crucially determine the usefulness of the portfolio process to teachers and to evaluators. If videotapes are used to give what appears to be a more "objective" look into a teacher's classroom, similar problems arise in the tension between the developmental potential of the taping process ("tell us what you see going on in your teaching") and the way that outside reviewers might bring judgments to bear on the tape, the reflection, or both ("he moves about too much during lecture").

Toward Responsible Assessment

We have thus far briefly explored just a few of the complexities that bear on the relationship between the developmental and evaluative functions of teaching portfolios. As we have tried to show, these general concerns are further complicated by the scholarly context of English and its allied disciplines. In such settings, faculty and administrators who use teaching portfolios to judge performance face unique challenges in their responsibility to create fair, uniform practices in the creation and interpretation of portfolios. We propose three such practices, each of which should be adapted to specific contexts in ways best suited to the planned uses and audiences of the teaching portfolio.

An Emphasis on Faculty Development

A department that requires the preparation of portfolios without offering extensive opportunities for faculty development in this area can expect resistance and frustration. In our consultations on many campuses, we have encountered few faculty who are bewildered by the *idea* of a teaching portfolio. But this clarity soon gives way to apprehension as teachers consider what sorts of documents to include and how to prepare them. Discussion turns quickly to matters at the heart of all rhetorical choice: Who's the reader? What's the context? How high are the stakes? What will be done with my words? As faculty work in small groups to prepare a course syllabus for presentation as a primary document, ninety minutes disappear in a flash, and an all-day workshop starts to feel inadequate to address the many complexities of the portfolio's organization or individual entries' style, length, or contents.

Used ostensibly for evaluation, teaching portfolios can provide an excellent context for faculty-development efforts that involve every teacher in a department. But these efforts need administrative support and reward. They also need strong, clear leadership from the portfolio administrators or reviewers, who should spell out precisely the goals of the program, the kinds of documents best suited for the occasion, and the way these documents will be read, evaluated, and factored into an assessment of teaching. As we will explain, being too specific about the precise criteria for evaluation can undermine a broader, more developmental program of portfolio development. But well before faculty actually submit their portfolio for review, it is crucial to provide them with such criteria.

Faculty-development efforts can bridge the gap between the formative creation of portfolios and their use in assessment. For example, faculty can spend time in workshops or meetings developing many kinds of entries, and then recommend certain entries to the administration for review. In this way, the portfolio does not become a mechanical process, but faculty still buy into the standards by which they will be judged.

Workshops should also explore extensively the difference between the genres of primary and secondary documents, with special attention to their interrelationships. A workshop focusing on the design of effective syllabi—even with the final goal of preparing one for a portfolio—usually raises fascinating questions about the language and tone of syllabi, what information is included, and what philosophy of learning underlies the design of the course. As faculty discuss their often tacit or unexplored reasons for certain decisions, these conversations become excellent starting points for secondary documents in which they present their syllabus to others (the popular "annotated" syllabus being one example).

An Emphasis on the Development of Evaluators

Many full professors of English will readily confess that they have little knowledge of higher-education theory or even of commonly used pedagogies; as committee members, they might be hard-pressed to reach judgment about a junior faculty member's portfolio entry that invokes active-learning strategies supported by theories of intellectual scaffolding, principles of classroom democracy based on the work of Shor, or the application of criterion- versus reader-based response strategies to students' papers as theorized by Elbow. With incomplete knowledge of such educational principles, portfolio evaluators are not unlike political science faculty judging the published articles of scholars in chemical engineering. The resulting frustration can lead to inappropriate stereotypes or the reversion to what the evaluator thinks he or she does, in fact, know: "Who cares about this bell hooks person—this teacher doesn't even know when to capitalize proper names!"

Of course, portfolio creators also share the burden of communicating their pedagogy effectively, and that will mean understanding the extent of their audience's knowledge. But without clear information about that audience, most teachers will forge ahead, creating potentially misunderstood documents for evaluators unschooled in the very arts they are judging.

To review portfolios competently, evaluators first need to be excellent, reflective teachers themselves, familiar with the major literature on teaching in higher education. They need to know, to take just one example, about the merits and limitations of lecturing, and about the research on students' attention during lectures and retention of information afterward. If a faculty member explains her methods for creating an active learning environment, the evaluator should know the theory behind these methods. The evaluator also needs to approach a variety of teaching styles and methods with enough objectivity to assess not *whether* a specific style or method is used but how effectively it works. Instead of discounting small-group work as "the blind leading the blind," a portfolio evaluator ought instead to look at how small groups are used in the classroom, and whether the teacher has reflected carefully on this use and/or actively assessed its value to students' learning.

Portfolio assessment works much better when several readers rate, discuss, and reach consensus on the merits of each portfolio. For example, a department can nominate and vote on a team of portfolio reviewers or members of a merit, promotion/tenure, or other evaluative committee who will serve for at least two years. As part of its work, the team or committee must engage in workshops, meetings, seminars, or other activities that focus strongly on the principles of instruction in higher education, perhaps tailored to the discipline. The team can then turn its efforts, for one or two academic years, to collectively evaluating the rest of the faculty's portfolios. Cycling new teams through a department in this way can create a "culture of teaching," where paying attention to students' learning matters, is evaluated, and is sufficiently rewarded. Every two years, the required contents of the portfolio can also be changed. This allows departments to focus more intensively on specific pedagogical concerns (integrating writing and speaking into coursework; dealing with issues of diversity; or learning more effective ways to work with reading).

Collective Formation of Evaluative Principles

Just as portfolio contents in a given year should be discussed and decided on collaboratively, *all* evaluative principles for judging these portfolios should come ideally from those being evaluated. Designing abstract principles may appear to work well (it's not difficult to come up with generalized standards for a "successful course design"), but in practice such ideals often fail. Instead, faculty must work from specifics first. Examining actual syllabi from past courses soon offers both basic and more subtle criteria for assessment.

For some colleges and universities, campuswide assessment practices can help to unite the faculty around the question of how to value and evaluate good teaching. Carefully formed interdisciplinary teams can successfully reach judgment about teaching on the basis of simple scales such as "exceeds expectations," "meets expectations," and "falls below expectations." Members of English departments and composition programs, for example, can present to faculty in the sciences portfolios that reveal and document their teaching methods, extra work with students, curricular development, and attempts to monitor and improve on their course evaluations. In some cases, introductions to portfolios in specific disciplines can acquaint outsiders with the typical methods used for teaching. For example, what might appear to be "pure lecture" to an English professor is actually, in higher mathematics, a "board-work" method of modeling the thinking processes used in the field. Or, as Sheila Tobias' experiments have shown, science faculty can't understand why a professor in a Chaucer seminar writes only one word on the board (1990). Knowing both the dominant teaching methods of a discipline and the ways in which those methods are being enhanced or supplemented can help outside reviewers to reach more careful, fair judgments of teachers' work.

Collectively determined principles for assessment can also help to foster a culture of teaching, especially one that encourages risk-taking. For example, a portfolio program can encourage faculty to include three documents in their portfolio that reflect active exploration of "problems" they perceive in their instruction. However, it is essential that the published criteria for the portfolio evaluation recognize these entries as exploratory and reward faculty for the degree of insight they display in working through particular problems. In more open-ended systems, where faculty have free choice about what to include, cover statements or "introductions" can help readers to understand the scope and nature of the portfolio.

Finally, criteria for evaluation are best accompanied by model portfolios in which teachers actively experiment with different media of display, investigate their teaching in systematic and even empirical ways, and offer insightful reflections that reveal their own "scholarship of teaching." Such models not only provide concrete evidence of certain criteria, but can help faculty to understand what is valued in the department or institution. Model portfolio entries can be placed on the departmental Website with hyperlinks, at strategic places, to annotations explaining how the published criteria are illustrated in the entries.

We conclude by strongly endorsing the use of teaching portfolios in a profession well prepared for their creation. Although we face significant challenges in adapting portfolios to the improvement of teaching in the humanities, this means of rich, authentic assessment promises to create departments abuzz with conversations, new ideas, and the sharing of what is often a strangely private activity. But to be effective, a portfolio program needs to be created carefully, over time, with attention to the voices of the faculty. Only through such collaboration can we achieve what Stephen Brookfield (1995) sees as the great strength of critical reflection, anchored as it is in "values of justice, fairness, and compassion" and finding its "political representation in the democratic process" (27).

10

Reading for Pedagogy: Negotiating the Complexities of Context from a Search Committee Chair's Perspective

Donna LeCourt

When I was searching for my first tenure-track job, the requirement to submit "evidence of teaching strength" appeared in no advertisement I saw. In fact, interviewers at MLA seemed surprised when I offered course proposals for them to assess. Now, a short eight years later, evidence of teaching strength in the form of teaching portfolios, syllabi, student evaluations, peer observations, and so on are commonplace. At my own institution, we request teaching materials for every search, and these materials are read as carefully as any other aspect of an applicant's file, frequently making the difference between whether a candidate is offered an initial interview or not. I, personally, have found such materials invaluable for getting a fuller picture of a potential colleague and appreciate the way this requirement reflects my institution's commitment to high-quality teaching. As helpful as such materials are in the search process, however, assessing such materials quickly presents a problem: how does one evaluate teaching outside of context?

Teaching portfolios frequently serve an evaluative function for a local audience (for example, the self, department colleagues, and so on), presenting an opportunity for the writer to reflect upon her practice within the teaching mission articulated by a given university. However, representations of teaching for a job search have no such identifiable contexts (see O'Neill and Mirtz in this volume). Rather, with the possibility of tenure-track employment at stake, candidates create portfolios so that teaching can be evaluated by an unknown audience whose purposes and contexts for reading are frequently as inscrutable as the faces of the committee. From the search committee's perspective, judging quality of candidates' teaching most often results in ranking and selection. As those of us in composition know, however, judging teaching quality outside of an institutional context or given course is extremely difficult. If reliable evaluative judgments of teaching practice are almost impossible to achieve in such a decontexualized space, then, we must ask, what function should/do teaching materials serve in the job search process?

In this essay I draw upon my experiences on nine search committees over the past eight years, and more specifically on two tenure-track composition searches (one as search chair) to attempt to answer this question. In particular, I highlight some of the reading practices I witnessed and participated in developing as a member of many search committees. Through a trial-and-error process of reading teaching materials together, my colleagues and I developed criteria and assessment processes that, I believe, helped us deal with this nagging issue of context. Based on these experiences, I suggest that while *practice* is extremely difficult to evaluate without reference to the teaching context, *pedagogy* may not be. Discussions and artifacts of teaching speak as clearly to a teacher's ways of thinking, making knowledge, and instituting scholarship in material practice as does evidence of research and scholarly potential (a criteria we are, as faculty, accustomed to assessing in job searches). This is especially true in composition. One of the unique and most satisfying aspects of our field is the clear link between our scholarship and material ends. We research in order to impact the material world, to produce knowledge that is applicable to the rhetorical situations of our classrooms and historical moments in society. This connection between theory and practice—pedagogy in its truest sense—is what, I discovered, I most hoped to see in the teaching materials of future colleagues.

Developing Criteria in Context

The process of developing criteria for assessing teaching materials was as beneficial for thinking about our program as it was for our future discussions of candidates. In previous nontenure-track searches, teaching evidence was ostensibly the most important and easiest part of the evaluation. When searching for lecturers to staff our program, I looked for candidates whose philosophy of composition was similar to our programmatic goals and whose teaching practices and strategies mirrored those we value. Although I hoped to find candidates with innovative approaches, I was more concerned with hiring colleagues who would support current pedagogical philosophies. Because their stays would most likely be short ones and the teaching loads are so heavy, I looked for someone who could successfully "hit the ground running" within our program.

What I quickly realized, however, was that assessing teaching materials for tenure-track searches would be a much different process. Looking for a clear "fit" with what we already do in our composition program is *not* what we are seeking in a tenure-track colleague. Rather, we hope to find candidates who are knowledgeable of recent scholarship in composition, can help us set directions for the program, and can institute curriculum for teaching assistants and nontenure-track teachers that will best meets our students' needs. Developing new criteria for tenure-track searches, thus, involved much conversation about our own institution, department, and composition program: what did our institution and committee value in teaching? How did we define "good teaching"? Answering these questions necessitated as much an assessment of our program as it did candidates' teaching materials.

This process involved several key elements of our institutional context. Colorado State is a Research I institution with a highly complex composition program. The composition program offers an M.A. in rhetoric and composition and an undergraduate writing concentration within the English major, and it oversees the curriculum and training of TAs and adjunct faculty for approximately 200 sections of first-year composition and 50 sections of upper-division writing that enroll students from throughout the university. Thus, the composition faculty teach a variety of courses—from graduate courses on composition theory to first-year writing—and participate in collaboratively administering the program, an active writing center (both physical and online), and a writing across the curriculum program. In such a context, we needed a colleague who could wear many hats, teach in a variety of situations, articulate principles of teaching practice in order to train others, and would be able to participate in constructing an ever-evolving vision of composition.

In addition to providing an opportunity for program assessment, developing criteria as part of the collective work of assessing candidates' teaching materials required me to make my own pedagogical investments public and open to scrutiny. I was forced to consider what our program ought to value in teaching, and thus what kinds of teaching practice our context demanded. Further, I had to articulate my own definition of "good" teaching clearly so that I could compare how that definition fit with my colleagues' definitions and their visions of the composition program. We began such conversations with *practice,* but quickly realized that we could not assess good practices from such decontextualized materials. Instead, we turned to more theoretical questions regarding *why* composition should be taught in particular ways. Individual opinions about what our program should emphasize—civic literacy, cultural studies, technological literacy, academic discourse, and so on—quickly came to the fore. Deciding upon one curricular direction, however, was impossible. Our program philosophy currently attempts to merge the best of all these approaches into a coherent whole. Since our current program philosophy was constructed through continual dialogue and dialectical encounters among our personal, scholarly investments, why shouldn't a candidate be given a chance to add to this mix rather than meeting a predetermined philosophical position?

Ultimately, we decided that assessing good teaching without substantial knowledge of the candidates' teaching contexts could only be done by assessing how well a given candidate is able to translate his scholarly investments into practice. His own scholarship could provide the context for the assessment. We did decide, however, that our current context also needed to play a factor in assessment. For instance, when discussing the "ideal teacher-colleague" in reference to administrative vision, I focused mainly on the need for new program directions. When conversations turned to immediate program need, I became just as concerned with how well a candidate would be able to collaborate with current faculty. Thus, we decided that "fit" still played a part in our assessment but more in terms of the ability to collaborate than replicate. This led committee members to identify shared commitments, a conversation that helped us define what remains the core of our program to this day: a focus on writing as a response to multiple rhetorical situations.

In this way, our committee's conversations proceeded dialogically, moving among the interrelated concerns of individual definitions of good teaching practice, individual and shared philosophical visions, the kind of teacher who could fulfill programmatic roles, and our immediate teaching needs for a new hire. From such conversations, we developed a set of criteria located in the specifics of our program and department that emphasized 1) a clear connection between research and teaching, 2) an ability to articulate the philosophy or theory that undergirds particular practices, 3) a teaching philosophy that might set new directions for our program, and 4) a philosophy that could be connected to, yet not replicate, our existing program philosophy.

From my perspective, these criteria fit our context well. A future colleague who understood intimately the connection between theory and her practices would best meet the needs arising from the contexts of our program and department. Rather than a certain kind of teacher, our program needed a teacher who could make knowledge about teaching and understand what guided her practice well enough to explain it to others. Given the complexities of our program, we concluded that teaching strength could best be determined by whether the candidate saw teaching as scholarship and scholarship as teaching, whether there was a dialectical relationship between these two bodies of work, and whether the candidate could examine the connections and disjunctions between her material interventions into teaching writing and the production of knowledge about writing. In sum, I assumed the self-reflective practitioner I valued so much when reading in-house teaching representations could also be assessed in job searches by looking for connections between a candidate's research and practice and examining the nature of those connections.

As helpful as the process of developing criteria was, the continual discussion of individual candidates initiated the more important conversation wherein the candidate's file represented an important voice in the conversation. It was frequently as a direct result of reading a particular file that I came to refine (in fact, decide) on our program needs. Our criteria, then, functioned to contextualize—

but not limit—our reading of candidates' files. Moreover, as individual candidates were assessed, our program was continually reassessed as well.

Although, ultimately, the criteria I brought to bear on candidates' files was still, necessarily, individual, they did not simply replicate either my own philosophy or my teaching practice, as my initial list did. Without the committee's discussions and the voices inherent in the candidates' files to temper my individual desires, I fear my assessment strategy may have easily resulted in valuing most highly those candidates who emphasized theory, showed an interest in cultural studies and writing for civic contexts, and used their reflections on practice to further help them enact these civic goals in writing administration and teaching. This is the danger in all searches—the tendency to assess the potential of candidates on the basis of one's own scholarly commitments. Such a danger is even more prevalent when assessing teaching. Much of the work we do as teachers is necessarily individualized—we develop our own curricula, teach out of sight of our colleagues, and institute our sense of composition within individualized classroom spaces. Many of the changes we make in these individualized classroom spaces also have the potential to alter a program's direction, yet more often than not we do not discuss them with our colleagues. Thus, the committee's collective commitment to and engagement with developing criteria not only ensured more equitable assessment of candidates' files but also strengthened our program. My colleagues and I were forced to make more public than we typically do our individual interpretations of the program and to assess more publicly and collectively possible future directions for the program, our consensus (or lack thereof) about where our program currently stands and most importantly, what the pedagogical philosophy of our program is or should be.

From such discussions, I was also able to develop a more dynamic approach to assessing teaching than that I had applied in previous, nontenure-track searches. This process exposed an important perspective that was missing from my earlier reading strategies: that the key to good teaching was not located in specific practices, but rather in how good teachers *think about teaching*. My primary question when reading files became: How does this candidate *think about* pedagogy—its connections to research, to theory, to a particular perspective on writing's possibilities and functions, *and* to institutional contexts—rather than the details of a particular course, a comment on a student evaluation, or a specific teaching practice. Rather than evaluate particular practices as "good" or "bad," or attempt to intuit how well a faceless teacher performs in front of a classroom of imaginary students, I now read teaching materials to assess whether a candidate thinks like the kind of teacher I value. At our institution, this kind of teacher is one who understands the multiple demands on teaching in terms of institutional and cultural contexts, one who engages his practice via theories and research in composition (his own or others'), and one who reflects upon his own teaching as a way of making knowledge.

Reading for Pedagogy

When reading files, then, I assume that a clear theory-practice link will tell me about the quality of a candidate's teaching and her potential to fill many of the administrative roles our program requires. Only after such assessment does my reading process move toward an *evaluation* of a candidate: could this candidate offer the program contributions I value? Could this candidate teach the program's courses? If I remain true to my desire to let the strengths of a given candidate determine my evaluation (and, perhaps, redefine my own assessment of our program needs), I need evaluation to be the final act of assessment.

When reading for pedagogy, I focus most obviously on how candidates' research interests connect with their teaching. Unfortunately, there is usually no single place within a candidate's file where such connections can be sought. The most logical place for a candidate to articulate connections between his teaching practices and his research interests is in the teaching philosophy statement that so often serves as a cover sheet for other teaching materials. Only rarely, however, have I found explicit connections between theory/research and pedagogy/practice in such statements. More often, philosophy statements have focused on specific strategies the candidate uses in class or on aspects of practice (for example, collaborative learning, student-centered discussion, peer response) that suggest a pedagogical philosophy but do not, by themselves, clarify what that philosophy is. Student-centered practices, for example, can take a variety of forms depending on how they are connected to the larger goals of the writing classroom. As a result, I hope to find an argument about pedagogy that addresses how the content and structure of the curriculum represents the teachers' larger professional commitments to the teaching of writing. What I am searching for is an explicit connection between the candidates' scholarly interests and their curriculum—what they teach and why—and how that can all be linked to *how* they teach.

Through reading files, I have learned that a lack of clear connection between the *goals* of a writing classroom in a larger context (that is, *why* we teach writing, what we hope students will do with writing when they leave our classrooms) and specific strategies does not mean that such connections are absent. There are understandable reasons why they may not appear in a philosophy statement. At many institutions, including my own, graduate students are supplied with curricula and allowed to adapt only specific practices to meet already determined goals. As a result, graduate students—even those in composition—are often inexperienced at describing their teaching in ways that point to a dialectical relationship between their specific commitments as researchers and the functions or purposes of writing they sponsor in their classrooms. Similarly, efforts to prepare job candidates for their move into tenure-track positions most often focus candidates' attention on the presentation of their research rather than a reconsideration of their teaching in light of new institutional contexts wherein they will likely be given much greater pedagogical authority for curricula. Thus, the kind of evidence I seek may never appear in philosophy statements, since many candidates assume the goals of their composition courses to be institutionally determined or so widely shared as to warrant little discussion. Further, our requests for "evidence of teaching strength" (the direct language of my advertisement) suggests that we seek evidence of *how* someone teaches rather than any discussion of *why* they teach in the ways they do. By making teaching a separate aspect of a job file, we imply that teaching and scholarship are two separate areas of assessment that need not (and perhaps should not) be explicitly connected. As a result, I do not hold the lack of such explicit connections in a philosophy statement against a candidate.

In assessing a candidate's understanding of how research and teaching connect, then, I look to other aspects of the file: the cover letter, dissertation abstract, and writing sample. Cover letters are particularly useful in such an assessment because candidates usually make explicit arguments about relationships between their scholarship, current teaching, and future teaching interests here. Likewise in writing samples and dissertation abstracts, candidates are often much more explicit about their theoretical and scholarly investments, providing me a kind of context for reading their teaching materials. Frequently, writing samples also make overt statements about the implications of research for pedagogy, since composition audiences seek this connection even in scholarship. No matter where I locate such connections, my task becomes using these contexts to reassess the candidate's teaching materials: are the kinds of issues and questions important to the candidate's research reflected in the syllabi offered? Are students being asked to struggle with or take on any of the complicated issues of writing that candidates point to in their scholarly work? A close reading of the syllabi goals' statements, student evaluations, or samples of student writing help me infer answers to such questions fairly easily.

When I began reading this way, glaring disjunctures were more apparent than I would have thought. For example, a candidate's research may examine complex theoretical perspectives on writing from multiple subject positions in a richly conceptualized public sphere while the teaching materials focus on academic discourse communities. Such a disconnect *may* point to someone who does not enact the research-practice connection I seek, but I also try to be cautious about coming to judgment too quickly. One problem with looking only at current teaching practice is the inability to tell if the goals of a given course were generated by the candidate or by the composition program in which she is currently teaching. When such a disconnect occurs, I search for proposed syllabi and/or statements in the cover letter. Many candidates, for example, will submit proposals for courses they would *like* to teach but have not yet taught or will detail in their cover letters the kinds of courses they hope to teach in the future. From these descriptions, I attempt to discern a theory-practice connection to their research that may not always be available from current curriculum.

Finally, in an effort to be as fair as possible, I consider whether the kind of research a candidate is conducting actually *can* be reflected in practice at this point. I understand that there are multiple reasons why practice and theory may not correspond seamlessly. Theory, after all, is not synonymous with practice. For instance, one's research may explore how people best interact in the material realms of writing, an investigation that may take much longer to work out in classroom practice than in research or theorizing. Such is frequently the case with my own work. In these cases, I again hope to see course proposals and/or a discussion of future teaching interests that may point to areas where such research might more fruitfully impact one's teaching, service, or community work.

From such reading processes, I can usually determine whether the kind of theory-practice connection I seek is present in a candidate's dossier and assess how well practice and theory align in a candidate's work. I must admit that the clearer connection I find, the more likely I am to evaluate that candidate highly, particularly if the candidate's work also seems like it could extend our program's philosophy in useful directions. Yet it is not complete coherence for which I am searching. Instead, I am hoping to assess something much more ephemeral: how does the candidate *think* about teaching? My focus on theory-practice is ultimately a search for a self-reflective practitioner within the context of her own materials. Absent reflections on successes and failures in actual classroom situations, assessing pedagogical connections between research and teaching helps me develop a picture of how this teacher thinks about (her) teaching as well as whether this potential colleague is in a position to use that knowledge administratively.

I emphasize the focus on "thinking about teaching" because my criteria and reading practices are not without their attendant problems. My assessment criteria could imply a reading strategy that presumes theory and practice can be seamlessly connected via pedagogy without all the complications everyday teaching practice brings with it (thereby privileging, in statements, the kind of coherence or unified self that Mirtz, Willard-Traub, and others critique elsewhere in this volume). Admittedly, this modernist search for coherence is in many ways unavoidable. I am attempting to "read" a person from a text, a reading strategy that itself suggests a single ethos or coherence of meaning inextricable from academic reading practices, which favor linearity, the assumption of the "man and his work," and clear development of a single line of argument. In sum, I read files as I read other texts in a scholarly context. Thus, I need to continually remind myself that what I am reading is *a* representation constructed for a particular context, and just as centrally, a representation that is constructed by *my* reading of the materials as much as by what the candidate has chosen to include.

Conclusion

I hesitate to draw direct recommendations from the assessment strategies I have chronicled here, since my reading for research-practice connections is so intimately tied to my institutional context. However, I do feel secure in offering to other search committee readers a series of questions that proved valuable, in my own context, for determining what our committee would value in the representations of teaching offered by job candidates:

- What does your committee and institution define as "good teaching"?
- How intimately is teaching tied to research in your institution's mission?
- What administrative roles, if any, do you expect a new hire to fill? What kind of teacher do these roles imply?
- Does your program have a coherent philosophy in place? What is that philosophy?
- Is your program searching for a colleague who will replicate certain practices or set new directions for the program? Is there a specific teaching philosophy you are hoping to add?
- How much flexibility is there in your criteria for assessing teaching via the candidates' dossiers? Do the criteria sponsor reading practices that allow individual committee members to fully engage with (and possibly be persuaded by) a candidate's pedagogical commitments (however different from the commitments currently defining the program/department)?

This list could go on, but the key is to generate questions for your committee that will make individual investments and programmatic assumptions open to scrutiny, thereby resulting in criteria that accurately reflect a shared program philosophy.

My single recommendation is that search committee members use the search process as an opportunity to improve not only one's faculty but also one's program. As a composition director and as a search chair, I have found searches to be one of the most fruitful sites for discussing program philosophy and future directions, since the stakes are so high. There are other venues for such program planning, of course, but rarely do the questions of programmatic change hit as close to home as when a group of colleagues considers hiring someone whose contributions and influence may last over the next thirty years.

11

The Ethics of Required Teaching Portfolios

Carrie Shively Leverenz

Like many rhetoric and composition faculty, I vividly remember my early days of learning to teach college composition. As a first-year teaching assistant at a large public university in the 1980s, my preparation amounted to a two-day crash course on the required curriculum, program policies, and grading. The only thing I can recall about these workshops was the extreme anxiety I felt when I had to grade a sample student paper. (I also remember a tense exchange between another new TA who announced that the paper deserved an F based on the number of errors and the writing program administrators who tried to persuade him to see some merit in the student draft. A few days later, the new TA quit the program.) Although the TA training that I experienced is no doubt familiar, in the last two decades writing program administrators have sought to improve the professional development of new teachers by increasing preparation prior to teaching, by strengthening support during teaching, and by developing means of evaluation that can lead to better teaching, not just ensure that teachers are meeting minimum expectations. For a number of composition programs, including the one I currently direct, requiring new teachers to prepare teaching portfolios is seen as a means of enabling both professional development and evaluation of teacher performance.

Teaching portfolios in this context typically require that teachers write a teaching statement, select materials that represent their teaching, and reflect on what those materials say about them as teachers. All three of these activities help teachers learn how to describe and evaluate their teaching behaviors, processes that contribute to a teacher's capacity for critical self-reflection toward improved teaching. Indeed, preparing teaching portfolios can be an occasion for setting goals and formulating plans for improvement (Seldin 1999). In addition, if teachers are invited to prepare these materials together, required teaching portfolios can encourage them to support each other through paired classroom observations, shared assignments, and responses to each other's teaching philosophies. The preparation of a teaching portfolio can also be an opportunity to work closely with a mentor, whether a faculty member or more experienced peer. As John Zubizaretta (1999) notes, "virtually all the literature on [teaching] portfolios advocates the collaboration of a mentor who helps guide the development of the process and who keeps the writer focused on how the portfolio improves teaching" (164). Finally, for graduate student teachers and those adjuncts who plan to seek full-time positions at some point, the preparation of a teaching portfolio gives them practice representing themselves as teachers. Although a teaching portfolio that is part of a job application should be constructed differently than one intended for evaluation within one's current program, there is still a benefit in developing the habits of gathering teaching artifacts, writing teaching statements, requesting letters of observation, and keeping track of student evaluations, since such habits are often required of full-time faculty.

Teaching portfolios have become an appealing tool for evaluation for many of the same reasons that writing teachers choose to evaluate portfolios of their students' writing. Required teaching portfolios also provide a structured means for WPAs to interact with teachers. In writing programs where I have worked, administrators do not interact with individual teachers beyond the initiation period unless teachers seek advice or unless external evidence—student evaluations or student complaints, for example—suggests that the teacher is in trouble. As an administrator, teaching portfolios allow me to concentrate my evaluative energy on a substantive representation of work that is submitted with enough time between evaluations for learning and improvement to occur, putting me in a better position to evaluate a teacher's progress. Portfolios also shift the burden of proof for good teaching to the teachers themselves, giving them more of a say in how they are evaluated by inviting them to reflect on and respond to evidence such as student evaluations and observation letters.

Despite these potential benefits of teaching portfolios for professional development and evaluation, when WPAs require teachers to submit teaching portfolios, they set into motion a number of ethical dilemmas, for both teachers and themselves. For example, many teachers worry about how to construct representations of their teaching that show themselves in their best light while also identifying areas for improvement. Similarly, many WPAs worry about how to respond to those representations both critically and supportively. Also challenging for the WPA is deciding how to use knowledge made in this interaction to create a writing program that is coherent and yet allows for and encourages difference. Indeed, this tension between a desire for coherence, sometimes understood as adherence to universal or overarching principles, and the desire to value difference characterizes many ethical debates in a postmodern age. How can WPAs make decisions that are informed by principles of right action but that also respond to inevitable differences between cases? How can WPAs develop writing programs that are based on what they believe to be best practices while remaining open to voices that dissent from or subvert those practices?

For most of the history of moral philosophy, philosophers have concerned themselves with the search for universal principles of ethics that apply in all cases. Although normative approaches to ethics continue to be pursued, such approaches have also been widely challenged, especially from feminist and postmodernist perspectives (Gilligan 1982, Noddings 1984, Ruddick 1990, Bauman 1993). In *Rhetorical Ethics and Internetworked Writing* James Porter (1998) identifies some key principles that a postmodern ethics might embrace. One, from the work of Foucault, is to see ethics as "a set of situated, constituted relationships rather than a static set of ahistorical or metaphysical standards" (52). Duties are immediate and shifting rather than universal. Another, from Lyotard, is the idea that each of us has "a duty to be 'obliged' in the context of local communities" (55). Porter also notes the importance of acknowledging the irreducibility of difference, a concept he gleans from the work of Luce Irigaray. As Porter concludes, "the celebration of diversity itself (in opposition against efforts to totalize or homogenize) along with the complication of subjectivity—is one of the chief features of postmodern ethics" (27). Porter, then, advocates a theory of ethics that is situated, relational, and that recognizes and encourages difference. This tension between a modernist or normative theory of right behavior and a postmodern theory of ethics provides one explanation for the conflict many WPAs feel between a desire for a coherent writing program that represents best practices in the teaching of writing and a commitment to value teachers' differences, including differences that lead the WPA to question her assumptions about what is "best."

When I assumed my current position as Director of Composition at a private, Ph.D-granting university with about 7,000 students, I made it a policy that graduate instructors were to prepare and submit a teaching portfolio each spring that would serve as the basis of a conversation with me about their teaching. (New instructors submit drafts of their portfolios at the end of the fall semester as well.) I hoped that requiring instructors to prepare teaching portfolios would encourage them to think in sustained ways about their teaching and how to represent it and would provide me with substantive data that I could use to effectively promote improvement in teaching on an individual basis. I also sold instructors on the benefit of preparing teaching portfolios by reminding them that they would have a head start on preparing materials for their academic job search. The required contents of this teaching portfolio include a teaching philosophy, a self-evaluation detailing efforts at professional development, syllabi, sample assignments, a sample student paper with teacher comments, a letter of observation from another teacher (graduate instructor or faculty), and student evaluations accompanied by a reflection interpreting the results. I developed these requirements around principles similar to those that inform the construction of writing portfolios. Teaching portfolios work best when they include a variety of evidence and when teachers have been asked to provide context for and to reflect on the significance of that evidence. I also thought it important that teaching portfolios include multiple perspectives on a teacher's performance—that of other teachers, students, and the teacher herself.

One of the first ethical issues to arise in requiring teaching portfolios was deciding who should be required to submit them. Currently, I require teaching portfolios only of graduate instructors, because those are the teachers for whom I, as Director of Composition, have primary supervisory responsibility. In addition to graduate instructors, the composition staff also includes a small number of adjuncts (typically fewer than six) and eight full-time instructors, as well as tenure-track faculty who volunteer for the appointment. I do not require teaching evaluations of faculty or full-time instructors because they are formally evaluated each year by the department chair. Adjuncts are not formally evaluated, though as the least connected members of the teaching staff, they may be the ones who would most benefit from the interactivity of preparing teaching portfolios and the support of substantive responses to their teaching materials. However, because of their low salaries, I have made participation in professional development activities voluntary rather than required. As Christine Hult notes in her introduction to *Evaluating Teachers of Writing* (1994):

> there are political and ideological reasons that make evaluating writing teachers a problem. The instructors who teach writing on college and university campuses are all too often marginalized groups: part-time lecturers or adjunct faculty hired for pitiful wages under deplorable working conditions or graduate teaching assistants exploited as cheap labor while they work on their advanced degrees. (3)

While writing program administrators may consider staff meetings, pedagogy workshops, and teaching portfolios as professional development activities, poorly paid, overworked teachers may have a hard time seeing the value of putting in those extra hours while student papers are waiting to be graded and the next class is waiting to be taught. Of course, a formal evaluation of teaching can be required of all teachers regardless of status on the grounds that all employees must be evaluated, but an ethical practice of evaluation provides some benefit to the person being evaluated. Although it might be argued that teaching portfolios are universally valuable, a postmodern approach to ethics recognizes that what might be deemed beneficial in one case would not be so in another. As David Schwalm (1994) suggests, the means of evaluating adjunct faculty should be determined locally based on a careful consideration of the adjuncts' working conditions (123). By inviting, but not requiring, adjuncts to attend workshops and submit a teaching portfolio, I hope I am offering them the opportunity to improve their teaching without the requirement that they submit to otherwise uncompensated hours of professional development. The moral ambivalence I feel in this case illustrates well the conflicts writing program administrators face as they seek to do the right thing in a world where there is no one right thing to do—and if there were, we could not know it.

An interest in ethics has been especially keen among qualitative researchers in composition who acknowledge the huge responsibility faced by researchers who use language to construct the "reality" of their findings (including the reality of research participants' experiences) and who thus bear special responsibility for the consequences of their research. A similar ethical dilemma is faced by WPAs who require teachers to construct representations of their teaching. If we understand that the representation of the experience of a researcher or teacher is constructed, toward what end does one construct that representation of experience? Much of the literature on evaluating teachers notes the important distinction between formative and summative evaluation. These different ends represent two very different rhetorical situations for the portfolio author. For most WPAs, who are in the business of supporting inexperienced teachers rather than of hiring experts, formative evaluation is typically much more important than summative evaluation. Graduate teaching assistants, for example, are given the opportunity to learn how to teach as part of their graduate training and rarely have their assistantships revoked except in cases of gross misconduct. Nevertheless, graduate students are keenly aware that any writing they do for someone in authority opens them up to a critique of their abilities. With apologies to Peter Elbow, there really is no such thing as an evaluation-free zone.

This question of representation and how that representation will be evaluated is perhaps most pronounced in teaching philosophies and self-evaluations. When I explain the required teaching portfolio to the teaching staff, I distinguish between these two documents by noting that a teaching philosophy presents one's beliefs about teaching, about what is to be taught and how. A self-evaluation, on the other hand, provides a critical interpretation of one's most recent performance, noting strengths and weaknesses, and identifying areas for improvement. The inclusion of both of these documents in a teaching portfolio creates an interesting ethical problem for teachers who may wish to articulate a belief in their teaching philosophy and question the efficacy of that belief in their self-evaluation. It can be difficult for new teachers, perhaps any teacher, to assert beliefs about teaching and at the same time turn a critical lens on their teaching. Another dilemma occurs for teachers who adhere to teaching philosophies different from those of their supervisors who will be evaluating their portfolios. One graduate instructor, who received his initial teacher training in another writing program, asked if he should say what he really thinks in his teaching philosophy, and I said, yes, only to find myself later advising him to *argue for* rather than simply *assert* his belief in the value of classical rhetoric to contemporary writing instruction, a value that is not emphasized in the program I direct. Would I have insisted on an argument from an instructor who expressed a philosophy more similar to my own?

More details about this particular case might make this ethical problem clearer. I knew from the grapevine that this teacher was frustrated at being asked to teach a curriculum not of his own devising. When he told me that he would not be able to attend required staff meetings because of a childcare conflict, we decided that he would communicate each week via email instead. Unfortunately, his physical absence from the staff meetings where new teachers were invited to question the common curriculum (his emails were perfunctory rather than critical) made it difficult for me to see his resistance and respond productively to it. I was thus taken aback when I read a comment on one of his student evaluations praising him for his teaching ability and sympathizing with the notion that he could have taught them a lot more if he did not have to teach the assigned curriculum. This teacher is clearly very good at teaching. His student evaluations are consistently high; his observation letters glowing. But he perceives that what he wants to teach is different from what I want him to teach. And I could not help feeling annoyed that he was criticizing the curriculum in front of his students without ever having talked to me about it. Ideally, the required teaching portfolio should be a place where such criticism could be expressed and responded to privately (without the audience of other teachers who were present at staff meetings), but neither his teaching philosophy nor his self-evaluation showed any evidence of dissatisfaction with the program. He did, however, create separate documents that evaluated the teaching workshops that I had conducted—and the evaluations were consistently negative. Perhaps this is one strategy he developed for being critical of the program without including such criticism as part of his self-evaluation. It was a sign that he separated his work as a teacher from what I perceived to be the work of the program.

Clearly, this teacher experienced conflicts about how to represent his teaching in relation to the program's goals. I, too, experienced conflicts as I thought about how to respond. I respected his different experience and perspective; yet I resented what seemed to be his dismissal of my experience and perspective. Ultimately, I wrote a response praising all the positive evidence in his portfolio but that also included the following paragraph:

> I guess I'm perplexed by the defensive tone you take throughout a lot of your materials. I now understand why one of your students said on his or her SPOTs [student evaluations] from spring that you could be teaching a lot if only you didn't have to teach what the program required, a comment which took me aback, as you can imagine. Your disagreements with the program curriculum seem to stem from your previous training and commitments, since those teachers new to the program do not have complaints about the curriculum. When I began my Ph.D. program, I had a lot of teaching experience and would have balked at being asked to turn my back on what I knew how to teach. At the same time, I learned a lot from working with other people who had different ideas than I did about the teaching of writing. That's all I'm asking from you—that you draw on what you know and believe about teaching writing but consider what I am offering as well.

I have no way of knowing how he responded to my response. He attended only part of the required presemester workshop this year and has not had a conversation with me since. Would we be on better terms if I had not asked him to represent his teaching and if I had not been provoked to respond to his implicit assertion of difference?

In another example of the ethical difficulties of representing one's teaching, a new teacher struggled in her teaching portfolio to represent herself as a competent teacher even though that competence had been challenged by her own self-reports in staff meetings, by her mentor's observation letter, and by her scathing student evaluations. Because my department chair asks me to read student evaluations before they are returned to teachers, I knew that students had said terrible things about her lack of authority, about her dress, about what they called her questionable grading practices. And I knew from other instructors that she had burst into tears upon reading these remarks. I expected, then, that her teaching portfolio, which included an analysis of student evaluations as well as a more general self-evaluation, might be a place where she could work through her response to what others had said about her teaching, allowing me to provide nonintrusive support for that work. While this teacher did mention several areas that she was working on improving, the emphasis was on what she had accomplished. Note the following example:

> I have grown better at defining standards of class behavior and enforcing them. Late in the semester, I still had failures in this area—some of them large ones. But I identified them more quickly and, instead of just lamenting my errors, began developing alternative courses of action. Sometimes this meant shifting to small group work instead of whole class discussion, if the class seemed particularly talkative and active. However, I didn't always catch my mistakes in time to do anything about them. On the day I had a student arrive half an hour late when he was supposed to give a presentation, I let him present. By the end of class, I realized that I had made a bad choice.

As a WPA, this kind of analysis is easy to praise. The teacher is attentive to her students' moods and adjusts her pedagogy accordingly. She makes a commitment to toughen up with slackers. But nowhere in her self-evaluation does she consider what she might be doing that allows students to get out of control in the first place. Even in her response to her students' negative comments about her teaching, she spends a good deal of time disagreeing with them. According to her, they were simply wrong about her clothing choices being inappropriate. Is there something about the rhetorical situation of the required teaching portfolio that led her to defend rather than interrogate her teaching practices? Although I read her teaching materials closely, I have no way of knowing whether she has simply constructed this positive representation for my benefit or whether she is in denial about what I consider to be serious complaints from students.

In another example of what might be called selective representation, a student came to me to complain that her teacher was not giving assignments like those her peers were being given. The teaching portfolio I had received from the teacher in the fall gave every indication that he was teaching the common curriculum, but the assignment sheets the student showed me from his spring semester class were clearly different. I called the teacher into my office and spent an exhausting hour arguing about the merits of his version of the course versus my version. I agreed with the student that this teacher's assignments were more difficult (or harder for students to engage with) than those in the common syllabus, but I also agreed with the teacher that he was teaching well and students were learning a lot. In the end, I told the teacher, "we're just never going to agree about what's best for students" referring to his choice of assigning topics for research papers and my choice of having students write from their interests. Is this teacher honestly free to represent his teaching in such a way that this kind of difference is made plain? My commitment to valuing difference led me to agree to disagree with this teacher, but not until we had both spent an exhausting hour in debate, and I had spent many more hours worrying about how to respond appropriately to both the teacher and student. Perhaps not surprisingly, this teacher chose to emphasize in his teaching philosophy the importance of accommodating his teaching to particular writing programs and their objectives, even as he continued to propound the benefits of the approach he honed before joining my program. While I respect this teacher's rhetorical savvy, I do wonder how to respond. On the one hand, I am tempted to question how serious he is about letting the writing program I direct affect his teaching practices. On the other hand, I remember my duty "to be obliged" to the teachers in this local context and to acknowledge the "irreducibility of difference" and so recommit myself to maintaining a conversation with this teacher in hopes that our differences will prove provocative and productive for us and for our students.

While I am committed to beginning my administrative work with the assumption that I am obliged to recognize and value teacher difference, not all differences are alike. For example, a teacher who wrote a policy on student plagiarism stating that the first incidence of insufficient citation would result in a conference with her and a chance to rewrite the paper (a policy that differed from the one I recommended, which cited a range of possible penalties) got herself into trouble when a student who blatantly cheated used her syllabus (interpreted by his lawyer) to keep from failing the assignment or the class. Ironically, her difficulty arose as a result of a policy that did not allow for differences in ethical action toward those who misuse sources in writing assignments. At the same time, I struggle to come up with common program policies on plagiarism or attendance or grading that are responsive to teachers' differing beliefs about those issues. I should note that this teacher did not have to submit a teaching portfolio, since she was out of funding and would not be returning to our program.

Her difference from the program, which had problematic consequences for her and for me, might not have been so problematic if it had been articulated and responded to.

Although these kinds of mismatches between what teachers are doing in the classroom and what I think they should be doing (or what they think I think they should be doing) is one kind of problem that teaching portfolios often fail to reveal—too close a match between teacher performance and my expectations is another kind of problem. One particularly thoughtful new teacher wrote the following as a journal response during a required course on Composition Theory, which she took with me during her first year of teaching:

> Berlin says "The test of one's competence as a composition instructor... resides in being able to recognize and justify the version of the process being taught, complete with all its significance for the student." This assertion makes me, as a new composition instructor, nervous. It does not make me nervous because I think it is a dangerous or faulty suggestion; it makes me nervous because I am not sure how well I understand my own pedagogy.... For one thing, this year I am using your syllabus and am following your teaching philosophies. This has unquestionably been a lifesaver for me, and I believe it has enabled me to teach students better than if I had developed a course on my own. I guess I feel like under this system the course can be successful even if I don't completely know what I'm doing.... This seems to go against what Berlin has said, though. He argues for intentionality in teaching, and last semester I was not all that intentional in my pedagogy.... I want to be able to know and to explain why I am teaching a certain way.... What I wonder, though, is whether I am really developing my own pedagogy or just learning more about yours?

And indeed, her teaching philosophy does bear a strong resemblance to my own, as exemplified by the common syllabus I wrote, and the pedagogical strategies I recommend. Although I can also read her teaching statement as a reflection of her own beliefs about teaching, I cannot help but wonder what it means that she has chosen in her second year of teaching to use wholesale my syllabus for Intermediate Composition, even though I offered it only as an example and invited teachers to come up with their own readings and assignments that will lead to the same general outcomes for students. Another instructor who is teaching Intermediate Composition for the first time announced that she, too, would be using my syllabus verbatim because she just did not have time or energy to invent her own. As an administrator who wants teachers to develop their own approaches to composition teaching, approaches that I hope they will share with me so that the common syllabus benefits from critique and revision, I am troubled by these teachers' unwillingness to represent their teaching as different from the writing program status quo. At the same time, I recognize that these teachers' introduction to teaching included a common syllabus and common assignments, which they dutifully submit in their teaching portfolios. Why, then, should "common" teaching philosophies concern me? Perhaps teachers believe that they are being evaluated on their faithful implementation of the course I wrote, a belief that obviously mitigates against the fostering and representation of difference.

In each of these cases, the tension between commonality and difference remains. And while I emphasize that required teaching portfolios are intended primarily for teachers' own professional development, teachers know that there is no such thing as formative evaluation alone when such evaluation is required and read by someone in authority. Like "freewriting" that is assigned and responded to by a teacher, a required teaching portfolio is also a performance; the audience and its expectations inevitably influence the performer who wishes for a favorable response. Indeed, since this essay will be included in my review for tenure, I am especially aware of the risk of representing myself in a way that might have negative consequences. Will my research seem too anecdotal? Will I be criticized for using the experiences of the teachers I supervise to advance my own academic career? Will my administrative philosophy come under fire? But such self-consciousness regarding how we represent ourselves as teachers and administrators and scholars is not all bad. All teachers need to learn how to see their teaching and their representation of that teaching as performances for multiple audiences: themselves, their students, their supervisors, their prospective employers. There is no one correct representation of teaching and no one ethical response to that representation.

Perhaps the most valuable thing about required teaching portfolios is the dialogue they can foster between teachers and the writing program. Assembling the portfolios requires teachers to think about their teaching in relation to what they imagine the writing program asks of them. Reading their teaching portfolios leads me to think even harder about what it means to have a coherent writing program that I can defend (as I am frequently called on to do) but that also encourages and values difference. This is especially true when I read the portfolios of those teachers who do not represent their teaching as I expect them to, when they avoid being openly critical of the program or when they evade others' criticism of them. When I ask myself whether it is fair to require teaching portfolios so that I can "read" the program and its instantiations across sections, I find myself answering, "yes," especially if doing so helps me to better support teachers rather than merely enforce program policies. When I had complaints from a few students about a teacher who, they claimed, did not know what she was doing, I was in a position to support her based on her strong teaching evaluations from the previous semester and her clearly articulated commitment to a transgressive philosophy of teaching heavily influenced by bell hooks. I was able to explain to students her rationale for what she was doing, making clear to them that she was meeting the composition program's expectations, and at the same time talk to her about how her challenging philosophy was being read by some students who expected a more authoritarian teacher not so emotionally invested in her teaching.

If Porter is right about the ethical necessity of such challenging work, teaching portfolios can become one means of making available for collective examination the tensions between commonality (or accommodation of writing program goals) and difference (or resistance to program goals). WPAs can demonstrate their commitments to this responsibility by developing reading and administrative practices that acknowledge the complexities of both the writing program as a local context and teachers' lives. As this chapter makes clear, however, both WPAs and teachers share responsibility for creating an atmosphere of collective engagement; and, both are to be valued for the way they make such tensions visible.

12

Building Community Through Reflection: Constructing and Reading Teaching Portfolios as a Method of Program Assessment

Ellen Schendel and Camille Newton

Teaching portfolios are, in part, exercises of power. Teachers write reflections on their teaching and construct their portfolios in the face of powerful pressure exerted through departmental expectations, disciplinary knowledge, the writing program's teacher education curriculum, and classroom experience. Because teaching portfolios are often constructed in response to these many (and sometimes conflicting) discourses, and because teaching portfolios meant to encourage reflective teaching practices are also often used in professional development and assessment decisions (to assign plum courses, give merit-based awards, or even rehire part-time faculty for another semester of teaching), we argue that the teaching identity constructed within a portfolio reflects the values of a department and the discipline at least as much as the values of the teacher. As such, teaching portfolios can become a means by which writing programs replicate existing theories and power structures.

This article makes two related claims. First, we argue that teaching portfolios should not be used within a writing program to encourage teacher development and to professionalize and assess individual teachers in the same moment. Development requires a "safe" and contextual environment for teachers to talk through what happens in their classrooms and perhaps to resist programmatic and disciplinary theories. Professionalization and assessment too frequently require teachers to construct an already-developed teacher identity, one that reflects and appeals to programmatic theories, practices, and disciplinary knowledge.

Second, we argue that because teaching portfolios provide glimpses into a writing program's values, using portfolios solely for teacher development or the assessment of individual teachers limits opportunities for engaging in program-wide assessments of curriculum and administrative policies. Instead, we propose a model of portfolio use based on the sharing of documents among teachers in a writing program. Such an assessment design capitalizes on the socially constructed nature of the reflections and classroom representations that make up teaching portfolios, focuses on the development of a writing program (rather than individual teachers), and allows for significant, productive change to occur as teachers contribute to ongoing discussions aimed at improving a program's curriculum.

Teaching Portfolios as Tools for Development and Professionalization

In general, articles and books about teaching portfolios celebrate their potential for teachers, writing program administrators, and teacher-educators. Peter Seldin (1997) argues that portfolios "enable faculty members to display their teaching accomplishments for the record . . . [and] contribute to more sound personal decisions and to the professional development and growth of individual faculty members" (1–2). Russell Edgerton, Patricia Hutchings, and Kathleen Quinlan (1991) point out that portfolios have the "potential for fostering the creation of a culture in which thoughtful discourse about teaching becomes the norm" (4). Such praise seems justified, for teaching portfolios can encourage reflective practice and offer teachers agency and participation in the evaluation of their teaching.

More recently, however, scholars have begun to register possible concerns about teaching portfolio use. Robert Yagelski (1997), for instance, cautions that teacher-educators should make careful choices about the design of their portfolio systems in order to address the tensions teachers experience in an evaluative context. He notes that student-teachers in his class were positive about their opportunities to document their development in a portfolio, but some were anxious (and even angry) as they attempted to do so for a grade in the class. Pearl R. Paulson and F. Leon Paulson (1997) concede that their student-teachers "discovered that the need to tailor a portfolio was influenced by how much personal risk could result were they to bare their own perspectives" (289). As one teacher in the class put it, " 'We are always striving to do what will please others even though it might have to be fudged to feel successful' " (289). Jon Snyder, Amy Lippincott, and Doug Bower (1998) found that it is desirable to use separate portfolios for development and credential purposes. Their study suggests "that efforts to combine the dual purposes of support and accountability in a *single* portfolio do not always result in constructive tension" (139, emphasis in original). And Carrie Shively Leverenz and Amy Goodburn (1998) warn teacher-educators about the problems with professionalizing teaching too quickly. They argue that if teachers are asked to present themselves as professionals for evaluation too quickly, they may focus on constructing a portrait of their teaching identity in lieu of studying and reflecting on their teaching in order to improve.

We support these emerging critical examinations of teaching portfolios and their use, recognizing the complicated nature of all assessments and identity constructions. More work needs to be done, however, to explore the power relations at work when a teacher constructs a portfolio. Many articles suggest that tensions between development and evaluation can be mitigated if the two purposes are more clearly separated and/or if teachers feel a sense of personal investment in and responsibility for the documents they include. Nona Lyons (1998), for instance, notes that "the portfolio process can be a compelling personal experience, offering an opportunity to reflect on one's learning and to articulate just who one is as a teacher." She sees the portfolio "as revealing a set of assumptions about teaching and learning, *ones shaped by a portfolio maker*" (4, emphasis added). Such accounts assume that teachers have significant autonomy and freedom in constructing portfolio identities. But postmodern theory suggests that identity construction is not a personal action, but rather a complex negotiation of discourses at work in a given context. Scholars such as Lester Faigley (1992) and James Berlin (1996) argue that institutional rituals and examinations—educational, economic, cultural, and religious—create subject positions for individuals, and it is only through negotiating these discourses that individuals can claim agency.

This view of identity compromises the claim that teaching portfolios can reveal developing teaching identities. Instead, portfolios highlight teachers' negotiations of the many powerful discourses at work in their teaching lives. Viewing teaching portfolios in this way opens up their uses and usefulness to a writing program. In this view, portfolios represent important and complicated intersections of values in literacy education—those held by individual teachers, a particular writing program, and composition as a field.

Portfolios in Practice

Many teachers have dealt with the discursive negotiations that teaching portfolios require. For instance, when one of our colleagues, an adjunct writing instructor at a state university, learned of a new programmatic teaching portfolio requirement, she was apprehensive—despite the fact that she was consistently recognized for her teaching and several times had been asked to mentor new adjunct writing instructors in the program. She viewed the teaching portfolio as a potential device for categorizing instructors in the program, and she feared her portfolio would not "measure up" to those of graduate students taking courses

124

in writing theory and pedagogy. She therefore obtained the syllabi for several graduate composition theory courses and read the required texts. She wanted, she said, to learn the terms and approaches valued by the department's faculty so that she could fashion her portfolio documents accordingly. Though praised by the faculty for whom she would develop the portfolio, this instructor did not think she had complete freedom to explore and justify her teaching identity; instead, she attempted to fashion an identity within the discourses valued by the writing program administration.

Several elements of this colleague's story warrant special attention. First, the requirement of a teaching portfolio motivated this teacher to delve into more scholarship about the teaching of writing. The teaching portfolio became an impetus to do more reading and thinking about how this teacher's theories and practices fit with those of the department and the discipline as a whole, challenging her to think more deeply about what she values in the teaching of writing. Second, this teacher negotiated many different discourses during the construction of her teaching portfolio: the theories and practices she read about, those that she saw and heard throughout the program, and her own teaching experiences. In this process, she came to understand more about what the writing program values. These are all positive effects of the teaching portfolio in and of themselves. But together, they tell an important story of how a single teacher in a single writing program constructs (rather than develops) an identity for evaluation, and how in such construction she rewrites and revises the field's values and those of the department. This colleague's experience illustrates the power of discursive identity construction in a teaching portfolio, power that is present not only for adjunct faculty being evaluated, but also for graduate students who are being "developed." What is missing, however, is a reciprocal relationship, a means for this teacher's inquiry and self-construction to impact the program in which she teaches.

As a graduate student, Camille completed a teaching portfolio for a composition theory and practice seminar. Although fairly new to graduate study in rhetoric and composition, she had been teaching college composition for more than ten years. She struggled to reconcile the varied theories of writing instruction she was learning and had been practicing, but she learned several things in the course: the department and course were decidedly social-constructivist in their approach; discussion of theory was emphasized and valued at least as much as discussion about practice; and teaching was viewed as a reflective, constantly developing activity. In order to ensure her success in the graduate program and in the discipline, and because she valued and respected the mentoring that the course provided, Camille wanted to impress the professor of the course, a rhetoric and composition specialist. She accordingly chose to frame her teaching philosophy with one of the assigned articles in the course, which theoretically "mapped" the field of rhetoric and composition. She foregrounded theory in her reading journal (mentioning her teaching practice only in relation to readings about theory) and she revised a required teaching narrative to include significantly more references to and discussions of composition theory. There is clearly nothing wrong with Camille's actions. The values of the professor and the department were aligned with current disciplinary values and conversations. But to suggest that the identity Camille constructed in the teaching portfolio for that course was personal or highly individual is inaccurate. Her portfolio reflects her awareness and accommodation of the discourses valued by the instructor and the department, not her own developing professional identity.

Such examples point to the need for greater attention to the power of discourses, and the consequences of such power for the continued use and reading of teaching portfolios. These accounts also suggest that teaching portfolios might be less suited to the assessment of individual instructors than to the assessment of how teachers' values and experiences (in writing classrooms, in the department or postsecondary institution more generally, in the field of composition and or English studies, and so on) shape a writing program.

Teaching Portfolios as Program Assessment

Program assessment is a growing body of research that seeks to support change within writing programs and universities. Paul Prior et al. (1997) write about program assessment as research "not defined by the usual dimensions—not marked by a particular methodological orientation, disciplinary affiliation, or object of study. For us, evaluation could best be understood as a category defined in terms of the contexts of research: the goals that initiate the research, its projected use, and consequences" (186). As research into the teaching and learning that happens within a writing program, it is "an ongoing activity that we engage in as reflective practitioners" (195), not simply a bureaucratic demand.

Yancey (1999) writes that program assessment represents an important development in assessment theory and practice because its focus on curricula and systems allows for (and even requires) different voices to be heard and different views to be considered for writing program improvement. This move toward improvement is perhaps the single most important characteristic of program assessment. Yancey and Huot (1997) make four "observations" about program assessment:

1. "As a mode of inquiry, assessment is increasingly collaborative and democratic," for program assessments rely on extensive data generation across broad groups of people with different interests and demands for writing instruction;

2. "Program assessment is a rhetorical enterprise" because it is the examination of the many discourses surrounding writing instruction and because it is an attempt to uncover many different narratives about writing assessment within a single program;

3. "Much of the learning produced in the name of assessment is very subtle in nature," because program assessments bring differing values to light, telling multiple stories rather than providing consistently clear answers to problems; and

4. "Program assessment is linked, directly or otherwise, to reformist agendas," for it becomes a way to propose changes, rethink curricula, and consider the way an entire system behind a program can be reworked in order to better attend to the needs of students, teachers, and administrators. (12)

Program assessments attempt to see the "big picture" (8), to understand how "learning and teaching ... interact so as to chart that interaction in order to understand how to enhance it" (10–11). In short, program assessments assume that change can occur and that teaching and learning can improve because of the various views that different groups of people bring to the table.

Program assessments, as Michael Williamson (1997) points out, are a means for reflective practice among teachers and program administrators: "[A program assessment] can provide an opportunity to sit back and reflect on what we are doing in our classes and how effectively we seem to be meeting the needs of our students" (256). When reflective practice becomes an integral part of what Cynthia Selfe (1997) terms "contextual assessments," or assessments that are constructed with the particularities of the local situation in mind and draw upon the materials and interactions generated from the many functions of a writing program, teachers can view themselves as "change agents" (53):

> [T]he methodologies of reflective teaching practice (Schon; Phelps) and contextual program assessment (Guba & Lincoln; Berlak et al.)—given that they involve participants in generating questions and concerns, carrying evaluation projects, and analyzing results—can make such understanding increasingly accessible at the level of consciousness and, thus, begin to take advantage of the intimate knowledge that social agents have of the situations within which they operate. (59–60)

Program assessments such as the type that Selfe advocates draw upon the work of teachers, putting the concepts of "change" and "reform" in a local context and in the hands of educators. Program assessment becomes an opportunity for greater understanding among all teachers and administrators within a program.

These attributes of program assessment—as an opportunity for reflection and learning, as a way for the many interests of a single writing program to be voiced and valued—resonate with the claims that scholars have made for teaching portfolios. Chris Anson (1994), for example, advocates that teachers share their portfolio documents in groups in order to hear what other teachers have to say about their theories and practices. These workshop discussions can lead to "revisions of primary [classroom-oriented] or secondary [reflective] documents [that] can then lead to changed attitudes and improved teaching strategies"(189). Yancey writes that "what we choose to allow in our model of [teaching] portfolio will not only affect the students (although that's true, of course), but it will also shape in crucial ways what we see and thus how we understand our own curriculum" (258). Yancey's point correlates with program assessment advocates' claims that generating documents in consultation with a wide variety of people with differing interests inherently values certain kinds of knowledge: hearing multiple stories, for example, rather than valuing a simple statistical figure or linear narrative. And, just as the particular design of a teaching portfolio assessment "shape[s] in crucial ways what we see and thus how we understand our own curriculum," so also does the particular design of a program assessment: Will students have their voices heard? Will teachers have the opportunity to talk with each other as part of the assessment, or will their responses be sought in isolation from one another?

Program assessment capitalizes on the constructed nature of teaching portfolios valuing the critical engagement that necessarily entails in the act of construction—critical engagement with systems and structures that produce knowledge, writing, behaviors, and subjects. Assessing writing programs is a way to ensure that the work that gets done by students, teachers, and administrators is directed toward a locally defined set of purposes—and that the products of the program's structure fit with the values and goals articulated by administrators and teachers. This concern with the local culture of a writing program is key. Because program assessments examine social interactions that comprise how writing is produced and valued by diverse groups within a program, they are tied to specific cultural values and needs. As Williamson makes clear, "evaluation research must serve the purposes of the participants in the writing program being examined" or the program assessment will not be valuable (245). The people who make up a writing program must be invested in the research process, for "quality assessment enriches the programs it attempts to describe and evaluate by increasing our understanding of curricula, teaching, and learning" (Huot 76). Just as a group of teachers reading each others' portfolios allows for reflection and change within their individual classrooms, reading teachers' portfolios allows for productive change to occur as teaching, curricula, and programmatic structure are considered in light of teachers' own words.

A Model of Portfolio Use as Program Assessment

Our vision for using teaching portfolios in program assessment is influenced not only by theory and scholarship but also by Camille's experiences with program evaluation at a large state university where she taught. To prepare for national accreditation review, the director of the composition program organized a writing program evaluation based on course portfolios. For each course in the writing program, teachers in the department were required to compile a course portfolio that included:

- The course syllabus
- All assignment sheets
- All handouts and materials distributed to students during the course
- Copies of sample student work (a collection of writing from three different students in the class representing low, high, and average work)
- An instructor's reflection, discussing course goals and assumptions, explaining and critiquing course materials, evaluating the success of the course, and detailing plans for teaching future sections.

The director of the writing program assured faculty and staff that the portfolios would be read anonymously and used to assess the program rather than individual instructors. Only by obtaining the master schedule of courses and deliberately linking teachers to course numbers could anyone identify individual instructors.

Once course portfolios were submitted, the director recruited teams of paid volunteers from the pool of teachers in the department. These teams read and discussed all of the portfolios for a single course and documented that work by taking notes and audiotaping reading sessions in which the group discussed:

- Common features or narratives about teaching that emerged in the documents
- Teaching practices, teaching materials, or reflections that troubled the team readers, indicating problems with departmental practices or individual teachers' responses to departmental goals and guidelines
- Individual teachers' reflections on common problems or concerns, particularly with respect to department guidelines, goals, or practices
- Evidence of excellence or areas of concern in teaching, and
- The fit between the department description and stated goals of the course and the teaching practices as described and documented in the portfolios.

The reading teams then submitted the audiotapes and notes with a summary letter to the department chair. When all materials had been submitted and reviewed, the chair sent a summary letter of the results to all participants.

Some significant flaws in this assessment design became apparent during the process of collecting and analyzing portfolios. Others became apparent only through reflecting on the assessment. First, perhaps because it was the first and only attempt at program assessment using portfolios in this department, many teachers worried that the department was using course portfolios as a means of surveillance (despite repeated assurances to the contrary). Second, although this method of program assessment allowed readers to learn from their colleagues' teaching and benefit from the multiple perspectives on a single course, only a few of the many instructors in the program were able to serve on reading teams. Third, the number of graduate students on reading teams significantly outnumbered the adjunct faculty, and the tenured and tenure-track faculty who participated were asked to read and discuss upper-division courses only, despite the fact that the majority of English classes were first-year writing courses. And finally, because reading teams focused on a single course, participants did not have an opportunity to learn via the assessment how that course might fit into the larger curriculum or connect to other courses offered by the department.

Despite these flaws in the design and execution of this assessment, however, there were a number of benefits for those participating. Team readers had the opportunity to discuss the goals of the course for which they were readers and to share sometimes very different views about the goals and structure of the writing program. Readers were able to learn from instructors who had very different approaches to the course and to discuss the value and significance of these divergent approaches. Once the department chair distributed the results of the assessment in a letter, teachers had the opportunity to explore how the data they had collected represented the course and the program as a whole, which encouraged them to evaluate the goals and practices of the course with respect to the goals of the program.

We believe this model of departmental assessment could be revised to address the problems and capitalize on the potential benefits associated with using teaching portfolios for program assessment. First, assessment could be undertaken more regularly. By "institutionalizing" the process—making it an annual event, for example—participants might come to see it as a regular occurrence rather than something to be feared for its unfamiliarity. Admittedly, institutionalizing the practice risks rendering it merely a matter of course, with little to no attention paid to the negative consequences it might have on the people participating in the process. In fact, too frequent an assessment might increase participants' anxiety, contributing to concerns that the assessment's ultimate function is regulatory and hegemonic. Therefore, some critical examination of the assessment itself is warranted as the assessment becomes routine. Such an examination might draw on anonymous surveys seeking feedback from participants; informal and formal discussions with reading teams about whether they find the assessment useful; and, careful attention to the formal and informal changes such an assessment might produce in a program—both the positive changes to curriculum it might suggest and the rumors it might generate about the administration's goals in sponsoring such an assessment process.

In addition to conducting program assessments more regularly, one might address some of the problems raised in the program assessment we have featured in this chapter by ensuring wider participation. Perhaps readers who make up the assessment teams could be rotated, so that everyone has the chance to focus on several courses (one at a time) over the span of a few years—and have the experience of reading with different colleagues each time. This practice is already in place in the portfolio grading groups at Grand Valley State University, where Ellen teaches. There, first-year writers are required to submit portfolios at the end of the term that are collaboratively graded by groups of faculty. Each group, comprised of adjunct and tenure-track faculty, meets approximately ten times during the semester to read and discuss student work-in-progress as preparation for grading the final portfolios and for learning about each other's classes before the grading takes place. Each semester, participants in the portfolio reading groups change. The intent of shifting participation is twofold: to encourage a sense of community among all first-year writing instructors by ensuring that each person works with different colleagues each term, and to allow each person's views to impact those of other teachers.

Adopting such an arrangement for reading groups in program assessment would have important benefits for the program. Discussing one's teaching with different people each semester could help individual participants develop their teaching in ways they might not have otherwise considered and sponsor across-the-program discussions of what ought to be valued in the teaching of writing. In addition, as instructors rotate through several reading groups across time— each focusing on a different course—they could gain a fuller understanding and offer back to the program and department knowledgeable accounts of how the curriculum fits together (or not).

A third recommendation that emerges from our work with the use of portfolios for program assessment is that those in charge of the portfolio assessment make sure that all instructors—tenured, tenure-track, adjunct, and graduate teaching assistant—participate not only as readers, but also as contributors of portfolios. Clearly a large task and a lofty goal, such a move would mitigate against any one group of teachers feeling singled out (or monitored). It would also establish the assessment process as well as the teaching of writing as something of value across the program, regardless of an individual's position or title.

Finally, the results of the assessment could be made more widely public, available to all teachers and interested students. The results of such assessment might be made available via the department's Website, the writing program's teaching suggestion files, or in placement information sent to students about the program's courses—indicating a culture in which all stakeholders (department administrators, teachers, students) are invited to contribute to programmatic improvement. In this way, the assessment might begin to cultivate suggestions for improvement that extend beyond curricular issues. The discussions instructors have within their reading groups, for example, might suggest topics for the GTA education course offered each year or for workshops sponsored by the writing program. Moreover, discussions about teaching begun in these small groups could help administrators to reenvision teaching positions in the writing program: the teaching load, the material conditions of teachers, and their compensation. In short, there are numerous ways participants' work through program assessment could be used to change a writing program's culture, curriculum, and structure.

Portfolio Authors as Change Agents

Kurt Spellmeyer (1998) has recently argued that it is time for our field to claim the power that rhetoric has within our departments, our universities, and our culture. Spellmeyer argues that composition studies is marginalized because of its concern with teaching; its lack of a core subject matter; its ability to forge connections between disciplines and between academe and community in ways that subvert the bureaucratic nature of the university. And he argues that these very characteristics of composition studies make it a powerful "anti-discipline," a force that can undermine the bureaucracy. Composition, as Spellmeyer sees it, is "the one venue within the university from which a genuine alternative might arise—an alternative to a hierarchy that thrives on fragmentation" (163). Composition can "break things into pieces, as so many of our colleagues like to do, but also to put them together again: to ask how different ways of seeing might converge within some larger whole, a whole presupposed by the nature of thinking itself" (164).

Spellmeyer offers an important argument about the possibilities for our field, one that calls on compositionists to construct new models for understanding the teaching of writing and new ways of "certifying" students, teachers, and writing curricula. To achieve its potential as an antidiscipline—an institutional force that builds connections throughout the bureaucratic university and between academe and community—composition must examine how its writing assessment practices and theories influence, undercut, or allow students, teachers, and administrators to "break down" and "put together" in meaningful ways the many elements that compose writing in the academy and the culture at large. Assessing "systems" is, in fact, the goal of program assessments. We believe assessments that rely upon department-wide readings of teaching portfolios are best suited to "break down" and "put together" the theories, practices, and interactions that make up a writing program.

13

Working Together, Advancing Alone: The Problem of Representing Collaboration in Teaching Portfolios

Stephen Fox

As I developed my teaching portfolio in the context of my university's promotion and tenure process, a question emerged that I have not seen addressed in the literature on teaching portfolios: how does one represent collaborative work in an individual portfolio designed for individual advancement? Advocates argue that using teaching portfolios will help make university teaching a more public activity that can be discussed, studied, and evaluated. They also encourage faculty to collaborate with others in compiling their teaching portfolios. But will faculty collaboration on the process of composing and evaluating teaching portfolios change the individualistic approach to teaching that dominates academic culture? Does collaborating on teaching portfolios necessarily encourage a view of teaching as a collaborative activity?

Academic work is collegial and collaborative more often than faculty in English Studies sometimes acknowledge. Researchers in the sciences and social sciences often work in groups and coauthor papers and articles; the humanities have had a more individualistic approach to research and writing. Composition/ rhetoric and linguistics are in this respect more like the social sciences, their faculty engaging in much collaborative research and writing. Also, those of us in composition and rhetoric have perhaps paid more attention to the collaborative dimension of faculty work than our colleagues in English Studies, partly because we have more often connected our research and our teaching—in fact, we have made teaching and learning the subject of much of our research—and partly because, as marginalized members of English Studies departments and the profession as a whole, we have been forced to consider and theorize our own work and our institutional situation. These differences within the field can create difficulties when faculty in composition or linguistics, for example, go up for tenure and promotion and their colleagues in literature and other humanities question coauthored work.

Even more difficulties arise because composition/rhetoric faculty engage in extensive work that carries not only the onus of being collaborative, but also the onus of not being published and thus not being recognized as scholarship. For example, writing program administration usually involves faculty working together to develop, implement, and assess curriculum; provide professional development for a diverse faculty teaching composition; develop placement procedures and assess their impact; and investigate the interaction between first-year composition and campus general education. In my own case, I have served on the Writing Coordinating Committee in my department ever since being hired. This committee oversees the first-year writing courses and our large part-time faculty. When writing a promotion and tenure statement or putting together a teaching portfolio for that purpose, I must work harder than those presenting a more typical research case to represent this work as scholarship—and to represent it as *my* work. I find myself needing to take credit for achievements that resulted from the hard work of the whole committee. The secret seems to be demonstrating that *my* contribution to that committee made a significant difference. It is not that I doubt the value of my contributions; but often it is difficult to disentangle individual efforts from such collaborative work.

Thus, two difficulties emerge. One, collaborative teaching in all its forms has to earn respect as scholarship, as work worthy of reward and worthwhile to undertake. Second, we have to find ways to represent such collaboration that will be recognized by our colleagues and our institutional structures.

Collaboration and the Individualistic Culture of the University

The individualistic ideology that drives the promotion and tenure process was highlighted for me in a conversation with a colleague. After reading a draft of my promotion and tenure statement, she noted how often I wrote in the first person plural and how often I referred to other people with whom I had worked. Valuing collaboration herself, yet being politically astute, she suggested that I substitute first-person singular and emphasize my efforts. After I revised the draft, we both agreed that the statement was stronger and would be more effective than the previous version. But I continue wondering whether I have clearly represented the collaborative nature of my work.

One could argue that using "we" or emphasizing the groups one has worked with obscures a faculty member's contributions, either diminishing them or ex-aggerating them. I am not arguing that a teaching portfolio used for a personnel decision should in some way be falsely modest or pretend to be other than what it is, an individual's report on an individual's accomplishments. But it seems to me that the promotion and tenure system itself and much of academic culture foster an overly individualistic, at times harmfully (and once in a while brutally) competitive atmosphere. Institutional structures and institutional culture affect the way we represent our work, including our teaching. The emphasis on individual achievement, on making one's scholarly reputation, especially affects junior faculty. M. J. Amey (1992) summarizes the findings of various studies that suggest that "the production orientation has worked to privatize faculty, isolating them in a narrow focus of inquiry which prevents them functioning as fully participating community members" (1628) and that "tenure rewards and breeds behaviors and characteristics that go against collegiality, the 'good citizen/loyalty to the institution' ideology of senior faculty—the same professors who set and increase the standards by which junior faculty work" (1629–30). One faculty member admitted that "once we get tenure, every self-seeking individualist act we have practiced professionally is validated" (1630).

Feminist scholars writing about academic work have noted this individualistic, hierarchical culture and its effects on women faculty in particular. In a study of collaboration among women faculty in women's studies departments, Cynthia Sullivan Dickens and Mary Ann D. Sagaria (1997) observe that collaborative scholarship "is not universally valued in the academy" (80). One of their study participants described collaboration as a "very feminist mode of work," in contrast with the hierarchical practices often found in the academy (93). Based on her own experience and that of survey respondents, Theresa Enos (1996) argues that collaborative scholarship is often devalued in promotion and tenure decisions (79–90). Again, it is not simply a matter of recognizing coauthored publications, for faculty in many disciplines (especially the sciences and social sciences) can make a good case for coauthored scholarship. For faculty in composition especially, it is also a matter of recognizing the scholarly nature of other collaborative work, such as writing program administration, curriculum design, and professional development workshops.

Collaborative learning has attracted more positive attention than collaborative scholarship. At my own university, we have had conferences, workshops, and in-house publications on collaborative learning; faculty from all disciplines are developing ways to make learning a more social, interactive enterprise, and group projects and small-group activities abound. We must now move deliberately to apply these principles to faculty work, especially teaching.

The Theory and Practice of Collaboration in English Studies

In recent years, literary scholars have worked to overthrow the Romantic, hero-worship approach to authors and authorship, seeing both the writing and the interpretation of literary texts as socially situated and constructed. Similarly, scholars in linguistics and composition have developed more social views of language development and use. W. Ross Winterowd and Blum (1994) observes that one characteristic of the "New Rhetoric" (the prevailing paradigm in composition studies since the early 1970s) is "the shift in rhetorical theory from the Romantic image of the writer alone in his or her study to the image of the writer as a member of a community or multiple communities, the writing as much a product of the community as of the individual writer" (48–9). James Berlin (1996) lauds research into collaborative learning and writing. Berlin summarizes this work on "text production within the context of collaborative learning" as interrogating "the insistence on writing as the exclusively private and personal act of a docile and quiescent subject" (174). I suggest that we apply these theoretical insights to our own faculty work, in particular our scholarship of teaching.

Perhaps few university professors would characterize themselves or their colleagues as "docile and quiescent," but we have certainly tended to view our work, including our teaching, as private, personal, and individual, and the way our work is judged no doubt has reinforced other influences in shaping our conceptions of teaching and the scholarship of teaching. Those of us in English Studies who practice and use research on the social and collaborative nature of textual and linguistic activity should logically apply these insights to our own teaching and the ways we represent that teaching. Teaching, after all, is highly situated within communities: the classroom itself is a community; as teachers we come to the classroom out of our disciplinary communities; and we sometimes conceive of our teaching as introducing students to those disciplinary communities and inviting them into disciplinary conversations. Teaching portfolios and dossiers are texts that represent subjects (ourselves as teachers), so we can interpret these texts with the same rhetorical theories and tools that we focus so adeptly on the texts that appear on our syllabi and in our scholarly articles and books.

Representing Collaboration in Teaching Portfolios

The issue of representing collaborative work in teaching—or, more broadly, representing teaching as collaborative work—has been dealt with only briefly or indirectly in published work on teaching portfolios. Sometimes the language used in this work reflects the individualistic view of teaching that I have noted above. For example, John P. Murray (1997) argues that the appraisal of teaching performance "must be individualized." Murray is arguing, rightly, against uniformity in assessing good teaching, and in that sense "individuality" or individualization is a valid goal. Yet individualistic conceptions of teaching disguise the collaborative nature of even the most innovative teaching and foster a heroic view of teaching often seen in Hollywood movies.

Those who have written about teaching portfolios usually talk about collaborating on the process of developing and evaluating teaching portfolios. Murray, for example, recommends that "administrators and faculty work together to develop the instruments and procedures" of evaluation. John Zubizarreta (1997) emphasizes the importance of collaborating with a mentor when developing one's teaching portfolio. In their AAHE monograph on the teaching portfolio, Russell Edgerton, Pat Hutchings, and Kathleen Quinlan (1991) also laud faculty collaboration in constructing portfolios: "Such collaboration is almost certain to be powerful where the aim is to improve teaching. When teaching is being evaluated for purposes of personnel decisions, faculty collaboration around portfolios might constitute a real sea change" (5). By implication, faculty collaboration around teaching itself should be seen as powerful and radical. Edgerton, Hutchings, and Quinlan draw this implication themselves in a later section, noting, "To treat teaching (and the development of the teaching portfolio) as a coached, collaborative activity is not to demean or undercut it but to raise its value and sharpen its practice" (51). Yet they go on to emphasize that encouraging collaborative work makes most sense "with high-stakes decisions out of the picture" (51). There's the rub. Even though some campuses encourage team teaching and collaborative service, when it comes time for personnel decisions, a highly individualistic approach is the norm.

Perhaps part of the problem is that collaboration in teaching does not always result in an easily identifiable product (like an article) labeled with the collaborators' names. Unless faculty are team-teaching, course syllabi have one teacher's name on them, even if that teacher has adapted the syllabi of colleagues, sought their input, or used a group-designed syllabus or set of assignments. The image of teaching as a solo performance persists. Lee Shulman (1998) sees this as a major stumbling block in having teaching viewed as scholarship. "Teaching is rarely evaluated by professional peers. And those who engage in innovative acts of teaching rarely build upon the work of others as they would in their more conventional scholarly work" (5). He also writes that "as teachers we experience pedagogical solitude, we are isolated and cut off from the other members of our professional teaching communities" (8). Many faculty in composition might argue that they are not so cut off, that in fact our field has been marked by a high degree of scholarly conversation within our professional teaching communities. Yet we would have to acknowledge that even within composition and rhetoric we often experience "pedagogical solitude"—our interaction with peers sometimes happens more at the disciplinary level, at conferences, and in journals, than at the campus or departmental level. And Shulman is right in arguing that we lack an accepted way of acknowledging the process of building on others' work and entering into a "conversation" about teaching a particular course or concept or skill. We do not document our use of others' work when it comes to classroom teaching, unless we publish an article or book about our teaching, and even then the matter of documentation is probably not uniformly agreed upon as it is with traditional "research." The use of teaching and course portfolios is spreading but is not yet recognized as a means of documenting and presenting teaching scholarship in the way that the journal article and monograph function for the scholarship of discovery. Even though teaching portfolios facilitate conversation about the scholarship of teaching, they are used more for evaluative than scholarly or curricular purposes.

Another problem when it comes to portraying collaboration is that the literature on teaching portfolios tends to focus on classroom teaching as the material for portfolio entries. What about the important pedagogical work that undergirds programs such as first-year composition, English as a Second Language, creative writing, or introductory literature? Faculty who work in such programs make important contributions to teaching through curriculum design and revision, program supervision, and faculty development. And these efforts are usually highly collaborative. They certainly are at an institution like mine, where the Director of Composition works with a committee to administer the writing program, and where directors of Creative Writing, ESL, Introductory Literature, and the University Writing Center meet regularly with other faculty to discuss curricula and teaching strategies. Other teaching-related work that is often collaborative and not always seen in sample teaching portfolios includes teaching committees, committees awarding teaching-related grants, and faculty groups doing professional development workshops and programmatic research. Reports from such committees and task forces often highlight group efforts, but when it comes time to represent the work in a dossier or teaching portfolio, the emphasis shifts to the individual's contributions, or the work is subordinated to more individualistic accomplishments. Another problem arises when such pedagogical work is viewed as service or administration, areas where collaboration is taken for granted and yet too seldom theorized or recognized as scholarly. Fortunately, scholars are beginning to examine and theorize such collaborative work; a recent issue of *Writing Program Administration* (Spellmeyer) explores the concept and practice of collaborative writing program administration, and Christine Hult (1995) has written about the scholarship of administration.

Representing Collaboration: My Teaching Portfolio

Because a promotion and tenure decision (or a decision to give a faculty member a teaching award or grant) does focus on one individual and affects his or her career more than anyone else, the first-person singular seems bound to loom large. Although I worked hard to satisfy readers' expectations that my dossier would represent individual achievement, I worked within the individualistic framework of the promotion and tenure process to represent my extensive collaboration with others in teaching, scholarship, and service. Before analyzing this representation, I need to explain briefly what my dossier included. My university requires a personal statement (a highly egocentric document!), a CV, and sections summarizing achievements in research, teaching, and service. Having chosen teaching as my area of excellence, I followed the precedent of several colleagues in my department and presented a teaching portfolio within the dossier's teaching section. This was not required, nor was it well understood by the school committee.

Many passages in my promotion and tenure statement highlight collaboration:

- I have asked my students and teaching colleagues to join me in investigating the assumptions and practices underlying the process of acquiring advanced literacy.
- I worked with a faculty group to further integrate new technology into our core writing courses; our efforts culminated in a successful grant proposal that enabled us to run a four-day workshop introducing many of our faculty to email, electronic library resources, and Internet discussion groups.
- For the past two years, I have been Director of the ITW Writing Project. . . . I have worked closely with my three codirectors, who work in schools in Mishawaka, South Bend, and Indianapolis, to bring this career-changing professional development program to elementary, high school, and college teachers of writing.
- Through these concentric circles of teaching activity, I have worked closely with colleagues in English and other disciplines and with many hardworking, dedicated students. I have made fruitful collaboration a hallmark of my style, and as a result made positive contributions to better teaching in the writing program, the English department, the campus, and the teaching profession in Indiana.

The first and last statements, appearing early and late in the essay, serve to frame the individualistic accounting in a collaborative context. I present effective collaboration as a key feature of my professional work and invite readers to share the assumption that such collaboration is one criterion for judging my work. Still, one can see the marks of the individualistic process I am engaged in. For example, I write, "*I* have asked *my* students and teaching colleagues to *join me*. . . ." The emphasis is on my initiative; I could have truthfully said, "My professional colleagues and my students have invited me to join them." But to advance in academe, one must emphasize originality rather than one's many debts to others.

I also tried to work within these constraints to highlight collaboration in my teaching portfolio, which was sent out for external review prior to being included in my promotion and tenure dossier. I followed Peter Seldin (1997) in organizing the early sections of my teaching portfolio, which opens with a reflective statement of teaching philosophy and practices. In a section of that statement about collaborative work in the classroom, I make this bridge to my other faculty work:

> I am convinced of the value of such collaborative work, despite its difficulties, because of the collaborative writing I do in my professional life. I have coedited a book that also involved coauthoring, coauthored a journal

article (about collaborative writing program administration, in fact), coauthored curriculum guides, and done joint conference presentations.

After this Statement of Teaching Philosophy and Practice, I included a Statement of Teaching Responsibilities (those are, of course, worked out collaboratively and, in my case, certainly involved negotiating my interests and the needs of the department), and a Summary of Student and Faculty Evaluation (including peer reviews by five faculty colleagues). I then presented a section on my work with the Writing Coordinating Committee, which I describe as "a collaborative faculty group whose collegiality and professionalism have contributed to making this program so excellent." Then, in a section on our first-year writing course, I move from my individual leadership, a catalyzing proposal I made, to group work on the course design: "I came up with the idea of designing a seminar on work. The other members of the Writing Coordinating Committee found this idea exciting, and a group of us developed a sequenced curriculum centered on this topic, piloted it, and revised it based on instructor and student feedback." Much of what I write about this course could be included in a course portfolio jointly authored by a half-dozen or more faculty.

In the portfolio section on teaching advanced expository writing, I refer to it as "our course" that serves English Education majors especially. I speak of my collaboration with other faculty who have taught the course, referring to myself as "a de facto coordinator of the course." Although this course does not have a common curriculum, those of us who teach it have shared syllabi and discussed goals and approaches.

In this same section, I also talk about what we could call "disciplinary collaboration"—my use of the National Writing Project model, my use of textbooks by Richard Coe and Peter Elbow, and my adaptation of an assignment developed by Tom Romano, who spoke at a conference I attended. Representing this kind of collaboration might help people see that teaching is indeed scholarship—that teachers enter into a scholarly conversation, and try to advance or use the conversation—and that disciplinary expertise undergirds the teaching being described. Such references to sources and influences would make dialogue about teaching easier and more fruitful at the disciplinary level.

Finally, in a portfolio section on "Contributions to Teacher Education," I discuss teaching-related work that goes on outside the classroom and that is highly collaborative. I discuss my work with the Indiana Teachers of Writing (ITW), a professional association that brings together teachers of writing at all levels, kindergarten through college. That work led to my directing the ITW Writing Project. In the portfolio, I write about working with my codirectors and teacher-consultants to maintain and develop our professional development programs. In a future version of my teaching portfolio, this work will be even more central, and I will need to develop ways to represent this collaborative scholarship of application and administration.

Conclusion: Future Directions

Perhaps teaching portfolios themselves, used rightly, will encourage more collaboration among faculty and a fuller recognition of the ways our teaching builds on and participates in the work of others. Course portfolios (see Hutchings et al. 1998) could be coauthored by two or more faculty who have worked together to develop and improve a course. I alluded to this possibility above, mentioning both a multisection course like first-year composition and a regularly offered course like advanced writing taught by different faculty over time. Certainly a portfolio representing our first-year writing course at IUPUI would need to be collaboratively written, and a group of us would take responsibility and whatever measure of credit was to be taken.

But there remains a disjuncture between any such collaborative venture or report and the individual faculty member's teaching dossier or portfolio. If the focus of attention is the particular course, program, or department, a collaborative portfolio should work as well as other documents representing group work and often authored by a group—for example, program and department self-evaluation reports prepared for external review. But when the focus of attention is the individual faculty member, especially one being reviewed for tenure or promotion, the connection between collaboration and individual achievement needs some elucidating. The individual faculty member up for review can attempt such elucidation in statements attached to the portfolio or in the portfolio itself. It would be helpful, though, for review committees themselves to discuss the role of collaboration in faculty work and develop better ways of evaluating such work. It would also be helpful for disciplinary journals and organizations to publish articles and sponsor conference and workshop sessions on documenting teaching and representing collaboration. When most of the discussion of teaching, documentation of faculty work, and redefinition of faculty work goes on in forums like AAHE, rightly or wrongly, many faculty will miss or ignore such discussion or relegate it to a lesser status than discipline-based scholarship.

Having said that, I will refer readers to Jon F. Wergin's (1994) thought-provoking AAHE monograph, *The Collaborative Department: How Five Campuses Are Inching Toward Cultures of Collective Responsibility.* Wergin summarizes his argument for collective responsibility:

> Our colleges and universities need to sharpen their priorities and focus their energies. But how can we do this as long as we continue to view academic departments as bands of individual entrepreneurs, pursuing professional self-interest, driven by discipline-imposed standards? Don't we need instead to begin treating departments and other academic units as self-directed *collectives* working cooperatively toward goals derived from a well-articulated institutional mission? Shouldn't an institution's performance incentives and rewards therefore focus on the departmental "team," and base faculty rewards on individual contributions to that team? (vii)

Wergin discusses the key issues raised by such a proposal. For example, colleges and universities have to balance the "collective good" with faculty autonomy (1–3); the "team" concept is not easy to apply in a university setting, for a "team" does not function in the same way as academic committees or departments (3–7); and ways must be found to "define, document, and evaluate individual performance . . . even in a team setting" (7). Wergin argues that universities and departments will have to develop "differential roles and expectations" for faculty, allowing individual faculty to negotiate different goals and allocations of effort as long as the department can fulfill its collective responsibilities (8–9). This will have to be done in ways that do not simply reinforce the existing individualistic "star" system or the hierarchies of value that diminish certain kinds of scholarship and faculty work.

Such far-reaching proposals reinforce the fact that how we represent our teaching cannot be divorced from the larger institutional culture within which faculty work. When thinking about collaboration in the context of teaching, I like the metaphor of conversation. What Tom Recchio (1998) says about writing program administration as conversational and relational applies to teaching as well:

> Within institutions relationships develop through language; thus, the quality of relationships within a writing program depends in large part on the quality of conversation . . . that the writing program stimulates and sustains (or not).
>
> Sustaining ethical conversation and thus relation within a writing program requires . . . a shift in emphasis from thinking about administration as masterful organization and implementation to conceiving of administration as relational and receptive. (160)

If we substitute "teaching" for "writing program" and "administration," we summarize a shift in thinking about teaching that has led to discussions about teaching as scholarship and teaching portfolios. To truly rethink teaching as relational and receptive, as stimulating conversation and sustained by conversation, would help us develop the notion of teaching as collaborative. We can represent our conversational, relational teaching in teaching portfolios, and those portfolios can become the basis for further conversation. Even the promotion and tenure process, or more broadly, the processes of faculty review, could become more collaborative and conversational, rather than rigidly hierarchical and secretive.

The metaphor of conversation distinguishes a promising development on my own and several other campuses: Campus Conversations on the Scholarship of Teaching, a program initiated by the Carnegie Foundation for the Advancement of Teaching and AAHE. At IUPUI, the faculty coordinator of the Campus Conversations, Richard Turner, professor of English, in his August 1999 Report to Colleagues, discusses teaching as a collaborative activity. Turner writes, "The scholarship of teaching regards teaching as part of the collaborative inquiry undertaken by faculty and students that drives the intellectual work of an academic community" (1). This notion of teaching as collaborative inquiry, and the emphasis on faculty collaboration with peers and students, recurs throughout the report. On a list of possible projects arising from the IUPUI Campus Conversations appears this promising suggestion: "Teachers would visit each other's classes and/or conduct small informal discussions of documented teaching work (i.e., course materials or course portfolios, teaching journals and case studies of important teaching occasions, or collaborative teaching initiatives)" (6). It should disturb us that such ideas seem new, even radical, but as Eileen Bender and Don Gray note elsewhere in the report, "we are curiously alone in our classroom and our reports on what we do are limited to anecdotes, the teaching itself is for the most part an extension of our personal vision, and the achievements of teaching are ephemeral" (7).

Again, I think it important that English Studies faculty find disciplinary (as well as interdisciplinary) forums in which to present, investigate, theorize, and discuss the scholarship of teaching, documenting such scholarship, and reconceiving faculty roles and rewards. Only then will we value such conversations and such work. For too long we have relegated serious discussion of teaching to Schools of Education, to K–12 teachers, and lately to faculty in composition and rhetoric. At least with the latter group, the conversation has pushed its way into the English department, sometimes into the center of the department, even into the chair's office.

In the concluding paragraph of his final book, James Berlin writes, "I thus want to make my last word a plea for collaborative effort. No group of English teachers ought to see themselves as operating in isolation from their fellows in working for change. Dialogue among college teachers and teachers in the high schools and elementary schools is crucial for any effort at seeking improvement to succeed. . . . We have much to gain working together, much to lose working alone" (180). To deal with the issue of representing collaboration in teaching portfolios, we can work on two fronts. First, we can engage in the kinds of collaborative efforts to improve teaching that Berlin and others advocate and that many of us have already been practicing. Second, we must find ways to *represent* this collaborative work in our conversations about teaching, including teaching portfolios and dossiers. We have to change the institutional mindsets and structures that too often blind people to the value of collaborative work; we have to create ways to evaluate teaching that are more collaborative and dialogic.

Works Cited

Alcorn, M. W., Jr. 1994. "Self-Structure as a Rhetorical Device: Modern Ethos and the Divisiveness of the Self." In *Ethos: New Essays in Rhetorical and Critical Theory,* ed. by J. S. Baumlin, and T. F. Baumlin, 3–35. Dallas, TX: Southern Methodist Univ. Press.

Amey, M. J. 1992. "Faculty Recruitment, Promotion, and Tenure." In *The Encyclopedia of Higher Education,* Vol. 3, ed. B. R. Clark, and G. R. Neave, 1623–34. Oxford: Pergamon.

Anderson, E., ed. 1993. *Campus Use of the Teaching Portfolio: Twenty-Five Profiles.* Washington, D.C.: American Association for Higher Education.

Anson, C. 1994. "Portfolios for Teachers: Writing Our Way to Reflective Practice." In *New Directions in Portfolio Assessment,* ed. L. Black, D. A. Daiker, J. Sommers, and G. Stygall, 185–200. Portsmouth, NH: Boynton/Cook.

Anson, C., and R. Woodland. 1997. "The Teacher Portfolio: A Tool for Teacher Research, Development and Assessment." Paper presented at the NCTE conference, "Conflict and Consensus: Exploring Diversity and Standards in the Portfolio Movement," 17 January at New Orleans.

Bakhtin, M. 1981. *The Dialogic Imagination: Four Essays by M. M. Bakhtin.* Trans. C. Emerson, and M. Holquist. Ed. by M. Holquist. Austin, TX: Univ. of Texas Press.

Ball, K., and A. Goodburn. 2000. "Composition and Service Learning: Appealing to Communities?" *Composition Studies* 28: 79–94.

Bartholomae, D. 1985. "Inventing the University." In *When a Writer Can't Write,* ed. M. Rose, pp. 134–65. New York: Guilford.

Bass, R. 1999. "The Scholarship of Teaching: What's the Problem?" Inventio. 1.1. *http://www.doiiit.gmu.edu/Archives/feb98/rbass.htm.*

Bauman, Z. 1993. *Postmodern Ethics.* Oxford, UK and Cambridge, MA: Blackwell.

Belanoff, P., and M. Dickson. 1991. *Portfolios: Process and Product.* Portsmouth, NH: Boynton/Cook.

Berlin, J. 1994. "The Subversions of the Portfolio." In *New Directions in Portfolio Assessment: Reflective Practice, Critical Theory, and Large-Scale Scoring,* ed.

by L. Black, D. Daiker, J. Sommers, and G. Stygall, 56–67. Portsmouth, NH: Boynton/Cook.

———. 1996. *Rhetorics, Poetics, and Cultures: Refiguring College English Studies.* Urbana, IL: National Council of Teachers of English.

Berthoff, A. E. 1981. *The Making of Meaning: Metaphors, Models, and Maxims for Writing Teachers.* Montclair, NJ: Boynton/Cook.

———. 1990. *The Sense of Learning.* Portsmouth, NH: Boynton/ Cook.

Bishop, W. 1991. "Going Up the Creek Without a Canoe: Using Portfolios to Train New Teachers of College Writing." In *Portfolios: Process and Product,* ed. P. Belanoff, and M. Dickson. Portsmouth, NH: Boynton/Cook.

———. 1999. *Ethnographic Writing Research: Writing it Down, Writing it Up, and Reading It.* Portsmouth, NH: Heinemann.

Black, L. 1997. "Reflecting on Course and Teacher Portfolios." Paper presented at NCTE Conference, "Expanding the Conversation on Reflection: Innovative Practices, New Understandings, Current Challenges," 26–28 June, at Montreal, Canada.

Bleich, D. 1995. "Collaboration and the Pedagogy of Disclosure." *College English* 57(1): 43–61.

———. 1998. *Know and Tell: A Writing Pedagogy of Disclosure, Genre, and Membership.* Portsmouth, NH: Boynton/Cook.

Blitz, M., and C. M. Hurlbert. 1998. *Letters for the Living: Teaching Writing in a Violent Age.* Urbana, IL: National Council of Teachers of English.

Bourdieu, P. 1990. *The Logic of Practice.* Trans. by R. Nice. Cambridge: Polity.

Boyer, E. L. 1990. *Scholarship Reconsidered: Priorities of the Professoriate.* Princeton, NJ: Carnegie Foundation for the Advancement of Teaching.

Britzman, D. P. 1994. "Is There a Problem with Knowing Thyself? Toward a Post-structuralist View of Teacher Identity." In *Teachers Thinking, Teachers Knowing: Reflections on Literacy and Language Education,* ed. by T. Shanahan, 53–75. Urbana, IL: NCRE, NCTE.

Brodkey, L. 1996. *Writing Permitted in Designated Areas Only.* Minneapolis: Univ. of Minnesota Press.

Brookfield, S. D. 1995. *Becoming a Critically Reflective Teacher.* San Francisco, CA: Jossey-Bass.

Bruffee, K. A. 1993. *Collaborative Learning: Higher Education, Interdependence, and the Authority of Knowledge.* Baltimore, MD: Johns Hopkins Univ. Press.

Burch, B. C. 1997. "Finding Out What's in Their Heads: Using Teaching Portfolios to Assess English Education Students—and Programs." In *Situating Portfolios: Four Perspectives,* ed. K. B. Yancey, and I. Weiser, 63–77. Logan, UT: Utah State Univ. Press.

Bush, L. 2001. "Teaching Philosophy. Teaching Writing and Literature On-Line." *http://www.public.asu.edu/~lauralou/teaching/teaching.html.*

Campbell, D., P. Bondi Cignetti, B. J. Melenyzer, D. Hood Nettles, and R. M. Wyman,

Jr. 1997. *How to Develop a Professional Portfolio: A Manual for Teachers.* Boston: Allyn and Bacon.

Carnegie Chronicle. 1999. "Scholarship Is the Big Picture," 7–9. Published under the auspices of the *National Teaching and Learning Forum* 8(4).

"The Carnegie Classification of Institutions of Higher Education." The Carnegie Foundation for the Advancement of Teaching. *http://www.carnegiefoundation.org/ classification/index.htm.*

Cazden, C. B. 1988. "Classroom Discourse." In *Handbook of Research on Teaching,* ed. by M. C. Whittrock, 432–63. New York: Macmillan.

Cerbin, W. 1996. "Inventing a New Genre: The Course Portfolio at the University of Wisconsin-La Crosse." In *Making Teaching Community Property: A Menu for Peer Collaboration and Peer Review,* ed. P. Hutchings, 56–8. Washington, DC: American Association for Higher Education.

Cochran-Smith, M., and S. L. Lytle. 1993. *Inside/Outside: Teacher Research and Knowledge.* New York: Teachers College University.

Council of Writing Program Administrators Outcomes Statement. April, 2000. Revised November 2000. *http://www.mwsc.edu/~outcomes.*

D'Antonio, A. 2001. Unpublished teaching portfolio.

DeZure, D. 1999. "Evaluating Teaching Through Peer Classroom Observation." In *Changing Practices in Evaluating Teaching: A Practical Guide to Improved Faculty Performance and Promotion/Tenure Decisions,* ed. P. Seldin, and Associates. Bolton, MA: Anker.

Dickens, C. S., and M. A. D. Sagaria. 1997. "Feminists at Work: Collaborative Relationships Among Women Faculty." *The Review of Higher Education* 21(1): 79–101.

Duffy, D. K., and J. W. Jones. 1995. *Teaching Within the Rhythms of the Semester.* San Francisco: Jossey-Bass.

Ede, L., and A. Lunsford. 1996. "Representing Audience: 'Successful' Discourse and Disciplinary Critique." *College Composition and Communication* 47.2 (May): 167–79.

Edgerton, R., P. Hutchings, and K. Quinlan. 1991. *The Teaching Portfolio: Capturing the Scholarship of Teaching.* Washington, DC: American Association for Higher Education.

Elbow, P. 1991. "Foreword." In *Portfolios: Process and Product,* ed. by P. Belanoff, and M. Dickson. Portsmouth, NH: Boynton/Cook.

———. 1998 (1973). "Writing Without Teachers." *English Education* 30(2): 75–152.

Enos, T. 1996. *Gender Roles and Faculty Lives in Rhetoric and Composition.* Carbondale, IL: Southern Illinois Univ. Press.

Faigley, L. 1992. *Fragments of Rationality: Postmodernity and the Subject of Composition.* Pittsburgh: Univ. of Pittsburgh Press.

Feiser, J. 2001. "Ethics." In *Internet Encyclopedia of Ethics. http://www.utm.edu/ research/iep/e/ethics.htm.* Accessed June 4, 2001.

Finkelstein, M. J., R. K. Seal, and J. H. Schuster. 1998. *The New Academic Generation: A Profession in Transformation*. Baltimore: Johns Hopkins Univ. Press.

Flannagan, A. M. 1994 "The Observer Observed: Retelling Tales In and Out of School." In *Evaluating Teachers of Writing*, ed. C. A. Hult. Urbana, IL: National Council of Teachers of English.

Fleischer, C. 2000. *Teachers Organizing for Change: Making Literacy Learning Everybody's Business*. Urbana, IL: National Council of Teachers of English.

Fontaine, S. I., and S. M. Hunter, eds. 1998. *Foregrounding Ethical Awareness in Composition and English Studies*. Portsmouth, NH: Boynton/Cook.

Foucault, M. 1982. *The Archaeology of Knowledge*. Trans. A. M. Sheridan Smith. *The Archaeology of Knowledge and The Discourse on Language*. New York: Pantheon.

———. 1990. *History of Sexuality, Volume 1: An Introduction*. Trans. R. Hurley. New York: Vintage/Random House.

Frank, C. 1999. *Ethnographic Eyes: A Teacher's Guide to Classroom Observation*. Portsmouth, NH: Heinemann.

Freire, P. 1968. *Pedagogy of the Oppressed*. Trans. by M. B. Ramos. New York: Seabury.

Gallagher, C., and P. Gray. 2001. "Ambivalent Reflections: On Telling 'True' Stories of the Classroom." *College Composition and Communication* 52(4): 651–8.

Gebhardt, R. C. 1997. "Preparing Yourself for Successful Personnel Review." In *Academic Advancement in Composition Studies*, ed. R. C. Gebhardt, and B. G. Smith Gebhardt, 117–27. Mahwah, NJ: Lawrence Erlbaum.

Gebhardt, R. C., and B. G. Smith Gebhardt, eds. 1997. *Academic Advancement in Composition Studies: Scholarship, Publication, Promotion, Tenure*. Mahwah, NJ: Lawrence Erlbaum.

Gilligan, C. 1982. *In a Different Voice: Psychological Theory and Women's Development*. Cambridge, MA: Harvard Univ. Press.

Glassick, C. E., M. T. Huber, and G. I. Maeroff. 1997. *Scholarship Assessed: Evaluation of the Professoriate*. A special report of the Carnegie Foundation for the Advancement of Teaching. San Francisco: Jossey-Bass.

Grimm, N. M. 1999. *Good Intentions: Writing Center Work for Postmodern Times*. Portsmouth, NH: Boynton/Cook.

Hamp-Lyons, L., and W. Condon. 1993. "Questioning Assumptions about Portfolio-Based Assessment." *College Composition and Communication* 44: 176–90.

Harris, J. 1997. *A Teaching Subject: Composition Since 1966*. Upper Saddle River, NJ: Prentice Hall.

Heiberger, M. M., and J. M. Vick. 1996. *The Academic Job Search Handbook*. 2nd ed. Philadelphia: Univ. of Pennsylvania Press.

Hillocks, G., Jr. 1995. *Teaching Writing as Reflective Practice*. New York: Teachers College Press, Columbia Univ.

Holquist, M. 1990. *Dialogism: Bakhtin and His World*. London: Routledge.

hooks, bell. 1994. *Teaching to Transgress: Education as the Practice of Freedom*. New York: Routledge.

Hubbard, R. S., and B. M. Power. 1993. *The Art of Classroom Inquiry: A Handbook for Teacher-Researchers.* Portsmouth: Heinemann.

Hult, C. A. 1994. *Evaluating Teachers of Writing.* Urbana, IL: National Council of Teachers of English.

———. 1995. "The Scholarship of Administration." In *Resituating Writing: Constructing and Administering Writing Programs,* ed. J. Janangelo, and K. Hansen. Portsmouth, NH: Boynton/Cook.

Huot, B. 1997. "Beyond Accountability: Reading with Faculty as Partners Across the Disciplines." In *Assessing Writing Across the Curriculum: Diverse Approaches and Practices,* ed. K. B. Yancey, and B. Huot, 69–78. Greenwich, CT: Ablex.

Hutchings, P., ed. 1995. *From Idea to Prototype: The Peer Review of Teaching (A Project Workbook).* Washington, DC: American Association for Higher Education.

———, ed. 1996. *Making Teaching Community Property: A Menu for Peer Collaboration and Peer Review.* Washington, DC: American Association for Higher Education.

———. 1998. *The Course Portfolio: How Faculty Can Examine Their Teaching to Advance Practice and Improve Student Learning.* Washington, DC: American Association for Higher Education.

———. 1998. "Designing Features and Significant Functions of the Course Portfolio." In *The Course Portfolio,* ed. P. Hutchings, 13–18. Washington, DC: American Association for Higher Education.

———, ed. 2000. *Opening Lines: Approaches to the Scholarship of Teaching and Learning.* Menlo Park, CA: Carnegie Foundation for the Advancement of Teaching.

Ives, M. 2000. "Writing Letters of Recommendation for Academic Jobs." *ADE Bulletin* 125 (Spring): 44–47.

Keig, L., and M. Waggoner. 1994. *Collaborative Peer Review: The Role of Faculty in Improving College Teaching.* ASHE-ERIC Higher Education Report No. 2. Washington, DC: George Washington Univ.

Lather, P. 1991. *Getting Smart: Feminist Research and Pedagogy With/In the Postmodern.* New York: Routledge.

Lee, A. 2000. *Composing Critical Pedagogies: Teaching Writing as Revision.* Urbana, IL: National Council of Teachers of English.

Leverenz, C. S., and A. Goodburn. 1998. "Professionalizing TA Training: Commitment to Teaching or Rhetorical Response to Market Crisis?" *WPA* 22: 9–32.

Lu, M-Z. 1999. "Redefining the Literate Self: The Politics of Critical Affirmation." *College Composition and Communication* 51.2 (December): 172–94.

Lucas, C. 1988. "Toward Ecological Evaluation." *The Quarterly* 10(1): 1–17.

———. 1992. "Introduction: Writing Portfolios—Changes and Challenges." In *Portfolios in the Writing Classroom,* ed. K. B. Yancey, 1–11. Urbana, IL: National Council of Teachers of English.

Lyons, N., ed. 1998. *With Portfolio in Hand: Validating the New Teacher Professionalism.* New York: Teachers College Press.

Moore, C. 2000. "A Letter to Women Graduate Students on Mentoring." In *Profession 2000,* 149–56. New York: Modern Language Association.

Mortensen, P., and G. Kirsch, eds. 1996. *Ethics and Representation in Qualitative Studies of Literacy.* Urbana, IL: National Council of Teachers of English.

Murray, J. P. 1997. *Successful Faculty Development and Evaluation: The Complete Teaching Portfolio.* ERIC Digest ED 405759. Washington DC: ERIC Clearinghouse on Higher Education.

Newkirk, T. 1997. *The Performance of Self in Student Writing.* Portsmouth, NH: Boynton/Cook.

Noddings, N. 1984. *Caring: A Feminine Approach to Ethics and Moral Education.* Berkeley, CA: Univ. of California Press.

North, S. M. 1987. *The Making of Knowledge in Composition: Portrait of an Emerging Field.* Portsmouth, NH: Boynton/Cook.

Ong, W. J. 1996. *Orality and Literacy: The Technologizing of the Word.* London: Routledge.

O'Reilley, M. R. 1998. *Radical Presence: Teaching as Contemplative Practice.* Portsmouth, NH: Boynton/Cook.

Paulson, P. R., and F. L. Paulson. 1997. "A Different Understanding." In *Situating Portfolios: Four Perspectives,* ed. by K. B. Yancey, and I. Weiser, 78–92. Logan, UT: Utah State Univ. Press.

Pemberton, M. A., ed. 2000. *The Ethics of Writing Instruction: Issues in Theory and Practice.* Stamford, CT: Ablex.

Phelps, L. W. 1993. "A Constrained Vision of the Writing Classroom." *Profession* 93: 46–54.

Porter, J. E. 1998. *Rhetorical Ethics and Internetworked Writing.* Greenwich, CT: Ablex.

Prior, P., G. E. Hawisher, S. Gruber, and N. MacLaughlin. 1997. "Research and WAC Evaluation: An In-Progress Reflection." In *Assessing Writing Across the Curriculum: Diverse Approaches and Practices,* ed. K. B. Yancey, and B. Huot, 185–216. Greenwich, CT: Ablex.

Rankin, E. 1994. *Seeing Yourself as Teacher.* Urbana, IL: National Council of Teachers of English.

Ray, R. 1993. *The Practice of Theory: Teacher Research in Composition.* Urbana, IL: National Council of Teachers of English.

Reagan, S., T. Fox, and D. Bleich, eds. 1994. *Writing With: New Directions in Collaborative Teaching, Learning, and Research.* Albany, NY: SUNY Press.

Recchio, T. 1998. "Writing Program Administration as Conversation." *Writing Program Administration* 21: 150–61.

Ritchie, J., and D. Wilson. 2000. *Teacher Narrative as Critical Inquiry: Rewriting the Script.* New York: Teachers College Press.

Robinson, J., and T. Singer. 1999. "Teacher Accountability: Setting Our Own Standards." *Centerspace* 13(3): 1–4.

Roemer, M., L. M. Shultz, and R. K. Durst. 1991. "Portfolios and the Process of Change." *College Composition and Communication* 42: 455–69.

Ruddick, S. 1990. *Maternal Thinking: Toward a Politics of Peace.* London: The Women's Press.

Ryle, G. 1949. *The Concept of Mind.* London: Hutchinson.

Salvatori, M. 2000. "Difficulty: The Great Educational Divide." In *Opening Lines: Approaches to the Scholarship of Teaching and Learning,* ed. P. Hutchings. Menlo Park, CA: Carnegie Foundation for the Advancement of Teaching.

Schell, E. E. 1996. "Portfolio." In *Keywords in Composition Studies,* ed. P. Heilker, and P. Vandenberg, 178–82. Portsmouth, NH: Boynton Cook-Heinemann.

Schön, D. A. 1986. *Educating the Reflective Practitioner: Toward a New Design for Teaching and Learning the Professions.* San Francisco: Jossey-Bass.

———. 1994. *Frame Reflection: Toward the Resolution of Intractable Policy Controversies.* New York: Basic Books.

———, ed. 1991. *The Reflective Turn: Case Studies in and on Educational Practice.* New York: Teachers College.

Schwalm, D. "Evaluating Adjunct Faculty." In *Evaluating Teachers of Writing,* ed. C. A. Hult, 123–32. Urbana, IL: National Council of Teachers of English.

Seitz, D. 1998. "Keeping Honest: Working Class Students, Difference, and Rethinking the Critical Agenda in Composition." In *Under Construction: Working at the Intersections of Composition Theory, Research, and Practice,* ed. C. Farris, and C. M. Anson, 65–78. Logan, UT: Utah State Univ. Press.

Seldin, P. 1991. *The Teaching Portfolio: A Practical Guide to Improved Performance and Promotion/Tenure Decisions.* Bolton, MA: Anker.

———. 1997. *The Teaching Porfolio: A Practical Guide to Improved Performance and Promotion/Tenure Decisions* 2nd ed. Boston: Anker.

———. 1999. "Self-Evaluation: What Works? What Doesn't" In *Changing Practices in Evaluation Teaching: A Practical Guide to Improved Faculty Performance and Promotion/Tenure Decisions,* ed. P. Seldin, and Associates, 97–115. Bolton, MA: Anker.

Seldin, P., and Associates. 1999. *Changing Practices in Evaluation Teaching: A Practical Guide to Improved Faculty Performance and Promotion/Tenure Decisions.* Bolton, MA: Anker.

Seldin, P., and L. Annis. 1992. "The Teaching Portfolio." *Teaching Excellence* 3(2).

Selfe, C. 1997. "Contextual Evaluation in WAC Programs: Theories, Issues, and Strategies for Teachers." In *Assessing Writing Across the Curriculum: Diverse Approaches and Practices,* ed. K. B. Yancey, and B. Huot, 51–68. Greenwich, CT: Ablex.

Shulman, L. 1993. "Teaching as Community Property: Putting an End to Pedagogical Solitude." *Change* 25(6): 6–7.

———. 1998. "Course Anatomy: The Dissection and Analysis of Knowledge Through Teaching." In *The Course Portfolio: How Faculty Can Examine Their Teaching to Advance Practice and Improve Student Learning,* ed. P. Hutchings, 5–12. Washington, DC: *AAHE*: 5–12.

———. 1998. "Teacher Portfolios: A Theoretical Activity." In *With Portfolios in Hand: Validating the New Teacher Professionalism,* ed. Nona Lyons, 23–38. New York: Teachers College Press.

Slevin, J. F. 2001. "Engaging Intellectual Work: The Faculty's Role in Assessment." *College English* 63.3 (January): 288–305.

Snyder, J., A. Lippincott, and D. Bower. 1998. "Portfolios in Teacher Education: Technical or Transformational?" In *With Portfolio in Hand: Validating the New Teacher Professionalism,* ed. N. Lyons, 123–42. New York: Teachers College Press.

Spellmeyer, K. 1998. "Marginal Prospects." *WPA: Writing Program Administration* 21.2/3: 162–82.

Sprague, J. 1993. "Retrieving the Research Agenda for Communication Education: Asking the Pedagogical Questions that are 'Embarrassments to Theory.'" *Communication Education* 42(2): 106–122.

Sproule, L., and S. Keisler. 1986. "Reducing Social Context Cues: Electronic Mail in Organizational Communication." *Management Science* 32(11): 1492–1512.

Strenski, Ellen. 1994. "Peer Review of Writing Faculty." In *Evaluating Teachers of Writing,* ed. C. A. Hult, 55–72. Urbana, IL: National Council of Teachers of English.

Teitel, L., M. Ricci, and J. Coogan. 1998. "Experienced Teachers Construct Teaching Portfolios: A Culture of Compliance vs. a Culture of Professional Development." In *With Portfolio in Hand: Validating the New Teacher Professionalism,* ed. by N. Lyons, 143–55. New York: Teachers College Press.

Tobias, S. 1990. *They're Not Dumb, They're Different: Stalking the Second Tier.* Tucson: Research Corporation.

Trimmer, J., ed. 1997. *Narration as Knowledge: Tales of the Teaching Life.* Portsmouth, NH: Boynton/Cook.

Turner, R. 1999. *Campus Conversations on the Scholarship of Teaching: Report to Colleagues.* Indianapolis: IUPUI.

University of Nebraska Peer Review of Teaching Project. *http://www.unl.edu/peerrev/*

Watzlavik, P., J. H. Beavin, and D. Jackson. 1967. *Pragmatics of Human Communication: A Study of Interactional Patterns, Pathologies, and Paradoxes.* New York: Norton.

Weingartner, R. 1999. *The Moral Dimensions of Academic Administration.* Oxford, UK: Rowman & Littlefield.

Weiser, I. 1997. "Revising Our Practices: How Portfolios Help Teachers Learn." In *Situating Portfolios: Four Perspectives,* ed. by K. B. Yancey, and I. Weiser, 293–301. Logan, UT: Utah State Univ. Press.

Wergin, J. F. 1994. *The Collaborative Department: How Five Campuses Are Inching Towards Cultures of Collective Responsibility.* Washington, DC: American Association for Higher Education.

Wiggins, G. 1984. "A True Test: Toward More Authentic and Equitable Assessment." *Phi Delta Kappan* 70(9): 703–4.

Williamson, M. M. 1997. "Pragmatism, Positivism, and Program Evaluation." In *Assessing Writing Across the Curriculum: Diverse Approaches and Practices,* ed. K. B. Yancey, and B. Huot, 237–58. Greenwich, CT: Ablex.

Winterowd, W. R., and J. Blum. 1994. *A Teacher's Introduction to Composition in the Rhetorical Tradition.* Urbana, IL: NCTE.

Yagelski, R. 1997. "Portfolios as a Way to Encourage Reflective Practice Among Preservice English Teachers." *Situating Portfolios: Four Perspectives,* ed. K. B. Yancey, and I. Weiser, 225–43. Logan, UT: Utah State Univ. Press.

———. 1999. "The Ambivalence of Reflection: Critical Pedagogies, Identity and the Writing Teacher." *College Composition and Communication* 51(1): 32–50.

Yancey, K. B., ed. 1992. *Portfolios in the Writing Classroom.* Urbana, IL: National Council of Teachers of English.

———. 1997. "Teacher Portfolios." In *Situating Portfolios: Four Perspectives,* ed. K. B. Yancey, and I. Weiser, 244–62. Logan, UT: Utah State Univ. Press.

———. 1997. *Assessing Writing Across the Curriculum: Diverse Approaches and Practices.* Greenwich, CT: Ablex.

———. 1998. *Reflection in the Writing Classroom.* Logan, UT: Utah State Univ. Press.

———. 1999. "Looking Back as We Look Forward: Historicizing Writing Assessment." *College Composition and Communication* 50.3: 458–503.

Yancey, K. B., and B. Huot, eds. 1997. "Introduction—Assumptions about Assessing WAC Programs: Some Axioms, Some Observations, Some Context." In *Assessing Writing Across the Curriculum: Diverse Approaches and Practices,* ed. K. B. Yancey, and B. Huot, 7–14. Greenwich, CT: Ablex.

Yancey, K. B., and I. Weiser. 1997. *Situating Portfolios: Four Perspectives.* Logan, UT: Utah State Univ. Press.

Zubizarreta, J. 1997. "Improving Teaching Through Portfolio Revisions." In *The Teaching Portfolio: A Practical Guide to Improved Performance and Promotion/Tenure Decisions,* 2nd ed., ed. P. Seldin. Bolton, MA: Anker.

———. 1999. "Evaluating Teaching through Portfolios." In *Changing Practices in Evaluating Teaching,* ed. by P. Seldin, and Associates, 162–82. Bolton, MA: Anker.

About the Contributors

Chris M. Anson is Professor of English and Director of the Campus Writing and Speaking Program at North Carolina State University. He is the recipient of numerous awards, including the Morse-Alumni Award for Outstanding Contributions to Undergraduate Education and the State of Minnesota's Teaching Excellence Award. His research interests include writing to learn, response to writing, faculty development, and the nature of literacy in and out of schools.

Rochelle Rodrigo Blanchard is a doctoral student in Rhetoric and Composition at Arizona State University. She teaches first-year composition courses in both traditional and multimedia supported classrooms. She has presented conference papers dealing with her research interest in the rhetorical and theoretical interfacing between teachers and students, as well as other people in general, and technology.

Laura L. Bush has a Ph.D. in English with an emphasis in American literature, autobiography theory, and computer mediated writing classrooms. She works as an instructional professional at the Center for Learning and Teaching Excellence at Arizona State University. Laura offers workshops and one-to-one consultations in strategies for teaching with technology, writing to learn, critical thinking, and constructing teaching portfolios, teaching philosophies, and curriculum vitae.

Lisa Cahill is currently a doctoral student in the Rhetoric, Composition, and Linguistics program at Arizona State University. She works in the Learning Center on the ASU East campus. Her research interests include Writing Across the Curriculum partnerships, as well as writing center theory and pedagogy. She is also interested in how new composition teaching assistants construct their teaching philosophies.

Deanna P. Dannels is an Assistant Professor of Communication and the Assistant Director of the Campus Writing and Speaking Program at North Carolina State University. Her cross-curricular work includes experience with faculty development, TA training, curricular revision, and instructional design. At the University of Utah, she was the recipient of a campuswide research grant for her work in oral communication across the curriculum, as well as a College of Humanities award for teaching excellence.

Amy D'Antonio is a graduate teaching assistant and doctoral student studying British Romanticism at Arizona State University.

Stephen Fox is Associate Professor and Associate Chair in the English Department at Indiana University Purdue University-Indianapolis (IUPUI). He is Director of the Indiana Teachers of Writing Project. He is coeditor of *Teaching Academic Literacy* (with Katherine Weese and Stuart Greene), and his work has appeared in *WPA*.

Anne Ruggles Gere is Professor of English and Professor of Education at the University of Michigan where she directs the Joint Ph.D. Program in English and Education. A former chair of CCCC and a past president of NCTE, she has long been interested in representations of teaching. Her most recent collection of essays (edited with Peter Shaheen) is titled *Making American Literatures in High School and College.*

Amy M. Goodburn is Associate Professor of English and Women's Studies at the University of Nebraska-Lincoln where she teaches courses in composition, rhetoric, and literacy studies and coordinates the Composition program. Her research has appeared in *JAC, English Education, WPA,* and in six edited collections. She was the 1999 recipient of UNL's "Scholarship in Teaching" award and currently co-coordinates UNL's Peer Review of Teaching Project.

Donna LeCourt is Associate Professor of English and Director of the Composition program at Colorado State University where she teaches courses in literacy studies, theories of writing, and cultural studies approaches to composition. Her work has appeared in *JAC, Computers and Writing,* and numerous edited collections. She was the 1999 recipient of the College of Liberal Arts' Excellence in Teaching Award. She is currently working on a book project on the body and identity politics in academic discourse.

Carrie Shively Leverenz is Associate Professor of English and Director of Composition at Texas Christian University where she teaches writing, composition theory, and cyberliteracy. Her research has appeared in *WPA, JAC, Computers and Composition,* and several edited collections. Her current book project is titled *Doing the Right Thing: Ethical Issues in Institutionalized Writing Instruction.*

Deborah Minter is Assistant Professor of English at the University of Nebraska-Lincoln, where she teaches graduate and undergraduate courses in composition and rhetoric. Her research has appeared in *College English* and the *Michigan Journal of Community Service Learning* and is forthcoming in *Literature and Medicine* as well as several edited collections. In 2000, she received the College of Arts and Sciences Award for Distinguished Teaching.

Ruth Mirtz is an Assistant Professor in the Department of Languages and Literature at Ferris State University in Big Rapids, Michigan. She teaches first-year writing, advanced composition, and linguistics, and she works with the Crossroads Writing Project. Her most recent work has appeared in the *Journal of Teaching Writing* and the essay collections, *The Writing Program Administrator as Researcher* and *The Online Writing Classroom.*

Camille Newton is a doctoral candidate in Rhetoric and Composition at the University of Louisville. She is currently completing a dissertation study of the students and texts in a Preparing Future Faculty program. Her research interests include graduate students' constructions of teaching and faculty identities, the preparation and evaluation of college writing faculty, and writing center development and administration.

Peggy O'Neill is Director of Composition and Assistant Professor of writing at Loyola College in Maryland, where she teaches a variety of writing classes. Her scholarship, which includes composition pedagogy, teacher preparation, and writing assessment theory and practice, has been published in journals such as *Composition Studies, Assessing Writing,* and *CCC* as well as anthologies. She is currently coediting two essay collections: *Practice in Context: Situating the Work of Writing Teachers* and *Field of Dreams: Independent Writing Programs and the Future of Composition Studies.*

Sarah Robbins is Associate Professor of English at Kennesaw State University where she teaches courses in English education, literacy studies, American literature, and women's studies. She is director of the Kennesaw Mountain Writing Project, a National Writing Project Site, and director of the Keeping and Creating American Communities program, a three-year initiative for community-based research on American culture funded by the National Endowment for the Humanities.

Julie Robinson is a doctoral student in Curriculum and Instruction with an emphasis in English Education at Arizona State University. She currently teaches first-year writing at Colorado State University and is finishing her dissertation, "The Coretta Scott King Awards: Motif and Meaning in Young Adult Novels."

Duane Roen, Professor of English at Arizona State University, served as Director of Composition for four years before assuming his current job of directing ASU's Center for Learning and Teaching Excellence. In addition to more than 130 articles, chapters, and conference papers, Duane has published *Composing Our Lives in Rhetoric and Composition* (with Theresa Enos and Stuart Brown); *The Writer's Toolbox* (with Stuart Brown and Bob Mittan); and *A Sense of Audience in Written Discourse* (with Gesa Kirsch). His current NCTE book project is *Strategies for Teaching First-Year Composition* (with Veronica Pantoja, Lauren Yena, Susan K. Miller, and Eric Waggoner).

Ellen Schendel is an Assistant Professor in Grand Valley State University's newly formed Writing Department, where she teaches academic and professional writing. Her scholarship, most of which centers on issues in writing assessment, has appeared in *WPA, Assessing Writing,* and *Computers and Composition.*

Tracy Singer earned her Master of Fine Arts degree in Creative Writing with an emphasis in Poetry at Arizona State University in 2001. As a teaching assistant, she taught freshman composition, writing for the professions, and introduction to poetry. She has copresented a model for constructing teaching philosophies at NCTE's "Teaching Teenagers to Write" and participated in a group-led roundtable and workshop on teaching portfolios at CCCC 2000. Tracy has also conducted community-based workshops for middle school and secondary education teachers on the topic of teaching poetry.

Margaret Willard-Traub is Assistant Professor of Rhetoric at Oakland University. She teaches undergraduate and graduate courses in writing and composition studies, and has published in the journals *Assessing Writing* and *Rhetoric Review.* She is a contributor to *Personal Effects: The Social Character of Scholarly Writing* (Utah State, 2001), and *Labor, Writing Technologies, and the Shaping of Composition in the Academy* (forthcoming). She is currently at work on a book project that brings together her interests in writing assessment and scholarly memoir, examining the practice and consequences of reflective writing by students and scholars across the disciplines.